Beginner's Guide
to Growing Fruit Trees Fast and Easy

Beginner's Guide
to Growing Fruit Trees Fast and Easy

Proven sustainable techniques for healthier trees and a bountiful harvest while reducing effort and time in planning, pruning, and maintaining them.

www.SophieMcKay.com

www.SmartMindPublishing.com

Copyright © 2024 Sophie McKay

Published in the United States of America, 2024

Legal Notice: This book is copyright protected. This book is only for personal use. All rights reserved. No portion of this book may be reproduced, stored in a retrieval system, or transmitted in any form or by any means – electronic, mechanical, photocopy, recording, or any other – except for brief quotations in a book review, without the prior written permission of the author or publisher. For more information, contact www.sophiemckay.com

First edition, 2024

ISBN 978-1-916662-18-6 (paperback)
ISBN 978-1-916662-19-3 (ebook)
ISBN 978-1-916662-20-9 (hardback)

Author's Bookstore: www.smartmindpublishing.com
Email: Sophie@sophiemckay.com
Author page: https://www.facebook.com/Sophie.McKay.Author
Facebook: www.facebook.com/groups/garden.to.table.tribe
Website: www.SophieMcKay.com

Table of content

Table of content 5
INTRODUCTION 11
CHAPTER 1 15
Getting Started With Fruit Tree Gardening 15
    Fruit Trees: A Smart Investment 15
    First Things First: The Basics 17
    Deciding What to Grow 19
    Understanding Your Orchard's Watering Needs 20
    Drainage: The Key to a Successful Orchard 20
    General Orchard Care 21
    Finding the Best Trees for Your Backyard 22
    It's All About the Sun 23
    Read the Land: Climate and Topography 25
    Know Your Zone 26
    Chill Hours 27
    Spoilt for Choice: Selecting Fruit Tree Varieties 28
    Tools, Equipment, and Resources 32
    Maintenance Tips 34
    The Takeaway 34
CHAPTER 2 35
Building Your Orchard Blueprint 35
    Designing an Efficient and Productive Garden Layout ... 36
    Orchard Layout and Design Principles 36
    The Plan: The Magic Formula 37
    Maximizing Sunlight Penetration 38
    Soil: Your Roadmap to Success 39

The Takeaway 42

CHAPTER 3 43

Planting and Establishing Fruit Trees 43

Selecting Healthy Fruit Tree Stocks and Rootstocks 43

Finding a Healthy Tree 44

Take Your Pick: Rootballed, Containerized, or Bare Root 49

Timing is Everything: Answering the When, Where and How ... 50

Staking: Protect Your Young Trees 53

Irrigation Strategies 57

Orchard Irrigation: Finding What Suits You Best? 58

Fruit Tree Nutrition 63

Step-by-Step Guide to Fertilizing Fruit Trees 67

Composting 67

Mulching 68

The Takeaway 69

CHAPTER 4 70

The Art of Shaping Trees 70

Training Vs. Pruning 70

General Guidelines for Training 72

General Guidelines For Pruning 72

Pruning Glossary 73

Thinning Cut 75

Heading Cut 76

Open Central Vs. Central Leader 78

Step-By-Step Guide to Pruning 79

Training Your Trees 81

Open Center Training 82

Central Leader Training 83

Espalier Training 83

Palmette 84
.Bringing Old Trees to Life 85
The Takeaway 87
CHAPTER 5 88
Organic Pest and Disease Management 88
Tackling Problems Head On 89
Inorganic and Organic Pesticides 92
Know the Enemy: Common Pests and Diseases 95
When Should You Spray? 99
Protect Your Orchard from Uninvited Guests 102
DIY Fence 103
The Takeaway 104
CHAPTER 6 105
Enhance Garden Productivity 105
Permaculture 105
Companion Planting 106
The Clover Solution 107
Guilding 108
Fruit Tree Guilds: A Blueprint 111
The Year-Round Harvest 114
Maximize Your Space: Grow in Containers 118
Grafting 120
A Guide to Grafting Fruit Trees 121
Grafting Techniques 123
The Takeaway 126
CHAPTER 7 127
Bring the Bees to the Yard 127
Pollination 128
The Who's Who of Pollinators 131

Nurturing Pollinators in Orchard Landscapes 134

Tips for Creating a Pollinator-Friendly Environment 135

Hand Pollination 137

The Takeaway 138

CHAPTER 8 139

Harvest Management and Winter Care 139

Thinning Top-Heavy Trees 139

Bringing in the Harvest! 142

Storing Your Produce 145

DIY Apple Storage Rack 146

Winter Care 148

The Takeaway 150

CONCLUSION 151

The Adventure Never Ends 151

Please Leave a Review! 152

Bibliography 154

Before we begin, go and grab your FREE gifts!

Sophie McKay's Seed Starting & Planting Calculator

+ The Ultimate Guide to Organic Weed Management

In these free resources, you will discover:

- The perfect Seed Starting and Planting times for YOUR region or zone
- The 8 Organic Weed Removal Methods
- The 6 best and proven Weed Management Methods
- The tools you did NOT know you need for a weed-free garden
- How weeds can help your yard
- How to identify which weed is good and which is bad for a yard or garden
- The difference between Invasive and Noxious Weeds

Get your FREE copy today by visiting:

https://sophiemckay.com/free-resources/

Ready for some more inspiration?

Check out Sophie's books to keep your garden thriving all year round. Create your own sustainable permaculture garden, or dive deep into container gardening with proven DIY methods for composting, companion planting, seed saving, water management and pest control! Learn how to grow your own food in harmony with nature. Success is guaranteed!

Sophie McKay's Easy and Effective Gardneing Series

Enhance Your Gardening Journey with Sophie's Garden Planners!

Just scan this QR code with your phone, or use the link to land directly on the book's Amazon page,

or

visit the Author's bookstore at www.smartmindpublishing.com

INTRODUCTION

It's harvest season! Time to put on my hat, grab a sharp pair of shears, slide a basket over my arm, and step into my backyard. So many fruits and vegetables are ready to be snipped off and taken indoors. Later, they'll show up on my dinner table as eggplant parmesan, stuffed bell peppers, and a tasty, homemade apple pie.

The kids dig up the potatoes, giggling as they push their tiny shovels in the dirt and squealing with joy when they find a plump potato lying snug in the soil. Later, they'll be in the small orchard behind the house, hunting blackberries from the blackberry bush, smiling triumphantly as they hold them up. In the kitchen, they watch with wonder as I wash and peel their spoils, turning them into their favorite foods.

As for dessert, the cherries, peaches, and plums are ready to be plucked and tossed into a fruit salad. By the time I return inside, my skin is flushed and glistening with sweat. I spread my harvest on my kitchen counter and admire the bright green vegetables and fruits I picked from my own backyard.

Ten years ago, I started taking steps toward sustainable living. My childhood memories of growing up on my grandparents' farm served as the stimulus for this change. I was driven by a desire to return to the simple life and quit the rat race, which could only be possible by ensuring food security for my family. Having my own backyard garden helped me achieve food independence and filled my life with immeasurable joy. I no longer had to worry about buying groceries, and could finally relax knowing I could prepare a delicious meal for my family any time from the fruits and vegetables I'd grown myself.

My first foray into gardening got off to a rocky start. The wilted lettuce, shriveled cucumbers, and wrinkled tomatoes almost made me give up. In hindsight, I'm so glad I didn't let those first few setbacks discourage me. Through perseverance and the right techniques, I eventually managed to create a flourishing vegetable garden. As fresh green vegetables from my home garden started making their way to my kitchen, I realized my kids didn't share my joy. They enjoyed fruits way more than healthy greens, so I embarked on my next venture: creating my own backyard orchard. However, it wasn't a decision I made overnight.

I was fraught with doubts and apprehensions. While I'd mastered the art of growing vegetables, I knew fruit trees would be an entirely different ball game. I was terrified of making costly mistakes, confused about pruning techniques, and afraid of dealing with pests and disease problems. Caring for fruit trees seemed like a time-consuming activity and I wasn't sure I could manage it.

After my first few years of growing fruit trees, most of my fears and worries melted away and I quickly realized that it was the best decision I ever made. Their dense canopy helped shield my shade-loving plants from the scorching sun while their thick bark protected fragile plant varieties from strong winds. Their blooms attracted swarms of pollinators, increasing overall garden produce. Soon my pantry became stocked with chutneys, jams, canned foods, and dry fruits so my family could enjoy their favorite foods no matter the season.

After the success of my first two books, The Practical Permaculture Project and A Beginner's Guide to Successful Container Gardening, I was brainstorming ideas for my next project when I glanced out my window at the rows of apple, cherry, fig, and peach trees growing tall in my backyard, the branches drooping under the weight of the fruits. The initial struggle I had to go through while planting them brought a smile to my lips as I reflected on how far I'd come.

As someone who firmly believes in sustainable, self-sufficient living, I want you to enjoy the experience of strolling into your orchard and plucking a plump tangerine or a ripe peach. I know how confusing it can be to choose what trees to grow. I understand how pruning may seem like a daunting task, and how challenging it can be to work with a small space. I've provided solutions to these issues and more in this book, so you could turn your dream into a reality.

I've packed this guide with all the information you need to get started on your backyard orchard in an easy-to-use format, so you have access to all the latest techniques and information. The book is divided into nine chapters dealing with a specific aspect of fruit tree gardening. You will learn the secrets of selecting the right fruit trees for your specific needs, creating the perfect microclimate, and maximizing yield to make the most of your limited space.

We'll start off our journey by understanding the basics in Chapter 1 before moving on to garden design and layout in Chapter 2. In Chapter 3, we'll learn how to find healthy fruit tree stocks and learn their care requirements. Chapter 4 covers pest and disease management through organic methods while Chapter 5 discusses pruning techniques. Chapter 6 lists fruit trees best suited for home gardens while Chapter 7 details advanced techniques to ensure year-round harvest. Chapter 8 includes important topics such as methods to increase produce, fruit load management, preservation, and autumn/winter care. Lastly, in Chapter 9 we discuss ongoing care of our orchards and how we can avoid running into problems.

Drawing upon my years of experience as a passionate gardener, I've carefully crafted this guide to empower busy individuals unable to fulfill their gardening dreams. I've compiled loads of smart techniques to cut down the time required to care for fruit trees while ensuring maximum productivity.

So, if you've ever dreamed of eating homegrown fruits but felt unsure about investing your time and energy into building a backyard orchard, it's time to let go of your fears and join me on the journey toward self-sufficiency. The patch of land outside your house is bursting with possibilities. This book will provide you the tools you need to uncover its hidden potential.

Imagine looking out your window at sun-ripened peaches, glossy red apples, and plums hanging from tree branches. Imagine going for an evening stroll into your backyard with bare feet, feeling the soft earth under your soles, picking a bright red apple off a branch, and crunching into it. All this can be a reality!

So, get ready to bring paradise to your doorstep.

CHAPTER 1

Getting Started With Fruit Tree Gardening

Getting Started With Fruit Tree Gardening

I love watching the trees in my garden in full bloom. During spring, my orchard is awash with color. The delicate petals drop a few weeks later, carpeting the ground. In another few weeks, the center of the blossoms bulges, growing bigger, changing color, and transforming into peaches, apples, pears, and other glorious fruits. Witnessing the entire process is nothing short of magical. Even after all these years, I'm filled with child-like wonder when the first few buds appear.

Ten years after embarking on my journey toward self-sufficiency, almost everything in my fridge is homegrown and homemade. It didn't take me long to realize that homegrown food is far superior in taste and quality to what is available in the supermarket. Once you've tasted the succulent peaches; crisp, juicy apples; and sweet, tangy plums from your garden, you'll hesitate going back.

The pleasures of fruit tree gardening are not limited to being a treat for your taste buds. Let's look at some benefits of growing fruits and the many ways they can elevate your home garden.

Fruit Trees: A Smart Investment

Having a backyard orchard gives you the freedom to grow your favorite fruits. Even something as common as an apple has thousands of varieties from which you can choose. Damsons, medlars, mulberries, and Japanese wineberries are some of the less common fruits I enjoy growing in my home garden. Such fruits are hardly ever on display at my local grocery store. With the right planning, you can have something new each month.

Initially, growing fruits may seem costlier than vegetables; however, you'll see massive returns on your small investment. The annual harvests will help you save money as market prices soar. The trees will stay with you for generations to come. Unlike vegetables, you don't have to plant seeds every spring and wait for them to grow. Since most fruits are perennials(they regrow every spring, unlike annual plants that grow for one season and die off), they require minimal care and are more capable of growing well without fertilizers.

Fresh organic produce at the grocery store is generally more expensive, making healthy eating a pipe dream for some. By growing your own produce, you can prioritize your health without sacrificing your wallet. With a fruit tree sprouting out of your yard, you can enjoy an abundant supply of delicious fruits without a hefty price tag. And if you end up with more than you can eat, you can always turn them into jams, sauces, and chutneys. The fruit goes directly from the tree to your kitchen, without a coating of wax and other preservatives. Moreover, you can opt for natural pest control instead of chemical pesticides, eliminating unnecessary chemicals from your food supply.

In addition to the health benefits, a backyard orchard can increase your property's value. Fruit trees are relatively easy to care for, add to the aesthetic appeal of the house, and may even reduce energy costs by keeping the home cool during the summer. And if you harbor an interest in bird watching, you're in for a treat! The eye-catching blooms and aromatic fruits will attract various bird species. You can even install a bird feeder and a bird bath to make these beautiful winged creatures stay longer.

As much as I adore my vegetable garden, it does not evoke the same happiness as my fruit trees. For example, my apple tree is the same age as my son. Knowing that I'd planted it a few months before my son was born makes me cherish it even more. When I see my son playing in its shade, my heart glows with joy. Soon, he'll be climbing its branches and picking fruit on his own. Growing along with you and your loved ones, fruit trees will carve a special place in your life, deepening your connection to nature.

First Things First: The Basics

It's tempting to dive into fruit tree gardening head first after learning about its numerous benefits. However, building a backyard orchard is a long-term commitment, so it's best to analyze the available space on your property and plan a rough layout. Before you jump into your car and head off to the gardening center to buy some fruit trees, here are a few things you need to consider.

Finding the Right Space

The success of your home orchard depends largely on providing your fruit trees with optimal conditions. Planting your fruit tree in the right space will set you off on the path to success. Here are some points you should consider to find the perfect spot for your fruit trees:

1. **Sunlight**

   Deciduous fruit trees (trees that shed their leaves annually such as apples, figs, cherries, apricots, pears, plums, etc.) need almost six to eight hours of direct sunlight. And while you can get away with a little less sun when growing tropicals and subtropicals like avocados and citrus, you may end up with smaller and fewer fruit. So finding a nice sunny spot is the first requirement of setting up your fruit trees.

   It's also important to consider that when the tree grows to its full size, it doesn't block sunlight for your other plants. For example, if you have a vegetable garden on the north end of your yard, planting a peach tree in the south may prevent sunlight from reaching the tomatoes, eggplants, peppers, and cucumbers when it's fully grown.

2. Space

It's important to anticipate the space requirements of mature trees before planting. Generally, larger varieties require ten to twenty feet (3-6 m) spacing while semi-dwarf or dwarf varieties may take as little as six feet (1.8 m). You may find the potential size of the tree on the tree tag when you purchase it and plant it accordingly.

Pruning also plays a huge role in determining the eventual size of the tree. I've got twelve trees in my garden that are spaced six feet (1.8 m) apart. I prune them from time to time, making sure their height doesn't exceed eight feet (2.5 m).

3. Soil

Well-draining, fertile soil is crucial for growing fruit trees. We'll discuss soil requirements in detail in Chapter 2; for now, here's a little test to determine whether or not the soil in your backyard has good drainage. Dig a small hole and fill it with water. If there's still water in the hole after an hour, then your soil has poor drainage. A 50/50 mix of compost and loamy topsoil managed to improve drainage properties of the heavy clay soil in my backyard.

You can also test the soil in your backyard by sending it to soil testing labs or using a soil testing kit like Redmond's Soil Test. Some labs in the US that accept mail-in soil samples include Colorado State University Soil Testing Lab, Crop Services International, and International Ag Labs. I did a Redmond's Soil Test for my orchard and learned that the heavy clay soil in my backyard had a high level of nitrate-to-nitrogen content, which can cause bushy plants, small fruits, and stunted roots. A soil test can also reveal the pH, level of salts, organic material, and nutrient concentration.

Here's a short questionnaire to help you find the best location for your trees. Carefully observe your backyard and ask yourself the following questions. Write down the answers on a sheet of paper and refer to it when choosing trees or positioning them in your backyard.

Observe and Question
The Sun • How many hours of sunlight does your location receive: full sun (6+ hrs), partial sun (3-6 hrs), or full shade (<3 hours)? • Remember that most fruit trees require six or more hours of direct light. • Some varieties such as pawpaw, Saskatoon berry, Cornelian cherry, and hazelnut can survive in partial shade.
The Soil • What kind of soil does your area have? • Is it well draining? • Does it contain healthy soil life such as earthworms? • Does it contain an adequate level of organic matter? • Is it rich in nutrients and minerals?
The Wind • Does your area get a lot of strong wind? • Does it receive chilly winds during the winter?
The Water • How much rainfall does your location get?

Deciding What to Grow

Tree selection may seem like a straightforward task, but requires a fair bit of planning. It can be broken into three simple steps starting with making a simple list of all the fruit trees you wish to grow on your homestead. At this point, there's no need to worry about whether the trees will grow in your area or not. Simply write down the names of the fruits you and your family enjoy.

Once you've prepared a list of fruit trees you want to see in your home orchard, it's time to hop onto the internet and find your gardening zone. The USDA Plant Hardiness Zone Map helps gardeners determine the plants best suited to their climate. Knowing your plant hardiness zone will give you an idea of which fruit trees you should buy. You can also talk to local gardeners to determine the varieties that will grow best, or consult with local nurseries.

Understanding Your Orchard's Watering Needs

Does your location have standing water for extensive periods of time? Is your area prone to heavy rainfall? Trees and fruit bushes will be a part of your landscape for a long time, so it's important to think about the weather conditions throughout the year and make necessary arrangements. For example, if heavy rain showers leave standing water on your property for days, building a rain garden near your orchard can help you avoid overwatering. A rain garden is simply a depression in the soil that collects and filters rainwater runoff. It allows water to slowly percolate into the soil (Winger, 2022).

Factors such as soil type, climate, local rainfall patterns, and your tree's watering requirements can help you estimate the amount of water you'll need. Once you've determined the above, you can choose an irrigation method to provide the correct level of moisture to your plants and avoid over or underwatering. Following a watering schedule can also minimize the risk of problems associated with inadequate watering. We'll discuss watering and irrigation strategies in greater detail in Chapter 3, so you can devise an irrigation system that caters to your orchard's specific needs.

Drainage: The Key to a Successful Orchard

Well-draining soil means water seeps into the ground, providing your plants with just the right amount of moisture. Low-lying areas near ditches, brooks, and ponds may be prone to becoming waterlogged. Moreover, most modern construction methods tend to degrade the subsoil (the soil lying under the surface or topsoil), leading to poor drainage. So even gardens that are not located in low-lying areas may experience waterlogging problems.

Generally, Loam or silt loam is considered the best orchard soil due to its excellent drainage and moisture-retaining properties. Clay soils tend to have the worst drainage properties and may lead to root disease. Meanwhile, sandy soils have poor water retention properties, requiring more frequent watering, which may result in the loss of nutrients.

Some areas may have a caliche layer present that must be penetrated to allow proper drainage. Caliche is a white or gray colored layer of soil, hardened by the accumulation calcium and magnesium carbonates. Depending on its composition, the layer may be hard or easy to break. Generally, soft caliche doesn't hinder root growth and development, although it may disrupt nutrient uptake. Hard, thick caliche layers affect plant growth by preventing the roots from penetrating deep into the soil.

A simple test to check the presence of a caliche layer on your land involves digging a one foot deep hole and filling it with water. If the water drains in four hours, the soil in your yard has adequate drainage. If the water takes more than four hours to drain, use a jackhammer to fracture the caliche layer.

General Orchard Care

A properly maintained fruit tree rewards its owner with an abundant harvest. While the mighty apple tree in your backyard doesn't require round-the-clock care, a few essential practices can help you achieve a superb harvest in the long run.

- *Mulching*: Adding a layer of mulch spread around the base of the trees can help retain moisture, inhibit weed growth, and regulate soil temperature. However, avoid placing the mulch directly against the trunk to prevent the risk of root rot.
- *Pruning*: Removing dead or diseased branches improves air circulation and light penetration, improving the overall health of fruit trees.

- *Fertilization*: Applying fertilizers provides the necessary nutrition to your fruit-bearing trees, ensuring bigger fruits and surplus harvest. Understanding the specific nutrient requirements of your trees can help you choose the right fertilizer although, in my opinion, organic fertilizers or compost are the best options available to home gardeners.

- *Pest and Disease Management*: Monitoring your trees for signs of pest infestations or disease can help you nip the problem in the bud and prevent serious damage. Using biological control methods and organic pesticides, you can help your plants recover and prevent future problems.

- *Harvesting*: Picking fruit off the trees at the right time is crucial for preserving the best taste and texture. Tying netting bags over the fruit before it's ripe enough for harvest can prevent birds and animals from nibbling at it.

Now that we've gone through a brief overview of what it takes to set up a backyard orchard, let's bring out our magnifying glasses and examine some of the most important points in more detail.

Finding the Best Trees for Your Backyard

It's time to solve the fruit tree puzzle and determine once and for all which trees should go in your orchard. As we discussed above, the clues lie in your backyard, but you may find them hard to decipher. Here's what you need to do to get to the bottom of this mystery:

Crack the Code: Evaluating Your Land

The key to a great home garden setup lies in keen observation and thorough planning. If you understand the space restrictions, sunlight patterns, and soil composition of your area, then you're off to a good start. Let's look at each component and discuss what you should be on the lookout for.

It's All About the Sun

Different areas in your yard receive different amounts of sunlight. Before you begin planting, study the amount of sun the area you've chosen for your orchard receives throughout the day. Is it covered in shade? Does it get morning or afternoon sun? Is it bright and sunny 24/7? Will any large trees or buildings in the surrounding area cast shadows on the spot you've chosen? And finally, what are the sunlight requirements of your trees?

Figure 1: A typical backyard orchard layout

You can easily find the sun requirements of the trees you plan to grow online, or check their labels at the gardening center. Fruit trees need a lot of sun while few varieties can manage in partial shade; however, a general rule of thumb to remember while setting up a home orchard is that more sun equals more fruit. Here are some terms to familiarize yourself with to understand to find the perfect spot for your fruit trees:

- **Full Sun:** These plants require six hours of direct sunlight per day for optimal growth. Most fruiting trees and shrubs fall into this category. Such plants are unable to survive in shady areas.

- **Full to Partial Sun:** Plants in this group prefer full sun but can tolerate some shade and partial sunlight. A minimum of four to five hours of direct sunlight coupled with dappled shade is required for the tree to survive; however, it may not produce as much fruit as it would in a sunny spot.

- **Partial Shade/ Shade Tolerant:** These plants do well in less sunlight, requiring only four hours or less of direct sun for healthy growth. They include a small number of fruiting plants as well as most leafy greens.

Placing sun-loving trees in a shaded area for long periods of time can have a disastrous effect. Telltale signs that a tree is not doing too well due to lack of sunlight include low fruit yield, leggy growth, yellowing leaves, and fewer flowers. Inadequate sunlight hinders photosynthesis, leading to low yield and lesser-quality fruit. Such trees are unable to defend themselves from insect and pest infestations and invariably succumb to a number of diseases. Here's a simple chart to give you an idea of the hours of sunlight that different fruit plants require:

Chart 1: Sunlight Requirements of Different Fruits

8 Hours	6 Hours	4 Hours
Apple Pear Cherry Fig Banana	Orange, Lemons Kumquats Grapefruits Tangerines Kiwi Grapes Peach Nectarine Plum Apricot	Berries Currants

Observing your garden or even your patio or balcony is critical to planning and selecting a good growing place. You can discover the optimum sites for trees and other garden equipment by spending time in your outside space and monitoring the patterns of sunshine, shadow, and wind. For example, if you see that one region of your garden receives full light for most of the day, you can plan to plant sun-loving fruit trees or shrubs there. If, on the other hand, you observe that a certain corner of your yard is always shaded, you can pick shade-tolerant variants that will grow in that setting.

Using these designs will help you maximize your available area and create a beautiful, healthy garden, regardless of how big or tiny it is.

Chart 2: Example of a garden-zone evaluation

Zone	Time			
	9 AM	11 AM	2 PM	6 PM
West wall	Shade	Partial sun	Very hot - full sun	Full sun
Vegetable garden	Partial sun	Sun	Sun	Sun
Apple tree area	Shade	Shade	Partial sun	Shade
South fence	Sun	Sun	Partial sun	Shade
Fireplace	Shade	Shade	Sunny - often windy	Sunny - often windy

Read the Land: Climate and Topography

Generally, citrus trees need a lot of summer heat and prefer frost-free areas. Apricots grow best in moderate climates while most berries such as raspberry, blueberry, blackberry, and strawberry flourish in cool coastal areas. If your region is exposed to strong winds, it's important to protect your orchard by installing wind barriers such as sturdy fencing.

Analyzing the topography of your landscape can give you a good idea about the conditions you'll have to work with. For example, the higher the land above sea level, the more exposed it is to weather fluctuations and cool temperatures. Dips and hollows in the landscape near your location can also influence the microclimate in your yard by collecting cold air. During winters, cold air sinks to the ground, flowing downhill and collecting at low points, forming frost pockets.

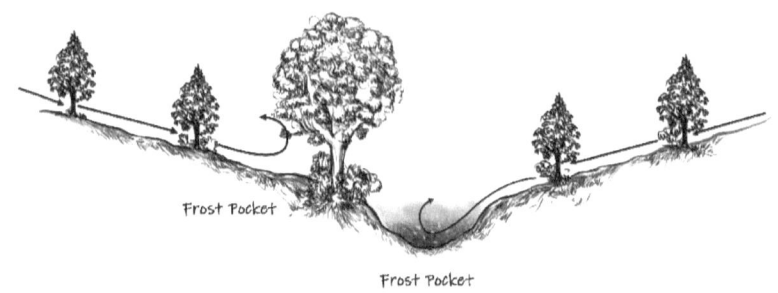

Figure 2: Formation of frost pockets in dips and hollows.

The formation of frost pockets in your garden may lead to late frosts in spring and early frosts in winter, shortening the growing season between the first and last frost. Cold air usually gathers behind fences or hedges on sloping land. Creating a few gaps in these barriers can drain the air, minimizing frost pockets.

In the northern hemisphere, south-facing areas soak up more light and warmth than north-facing. Fences and walls reflect warmth, which may cause trees in south-facing regions to heat up more quickly. This may prevent frost while promoting fruit ripening. North-facing gardens may get more shade but temperatures remain consistent throughout the day. East-facing gardens get more sun in the morning while west-facing ones enjoy more sunlight in the afternoons and evenings.

Know Your Zone

You'll often hear gardening enthusiasts use the term "hardiness" when choosing the right plants for a particular area. Hardiness refers to a plant's cold tolerance, while hardiness zones describe the climate of an area based on the lowest winter temperature recorded there (urban areas are usually warmer than the countryside, so take this into consideration). The 2012 USDA Plant Hardiness Zone Map is the gardeners' and growers' bible to find plants that will thrive in their location. The U.S. and Europe are divided into 13 climatic zones according to the U.S. Department of Agriculture Plant Hardiness Zone

Map. Zone 1 is the coldest including regions such as Alaska where the mercury drops to -50°F (-45°C), while temperatures in zone 13 hardly ever dip below 65°F (18°C). Zone 13 includes warm areas such as Hawaii and Florida. A simple trick for novice gardeners to avoid confusion is to remember that the lower the number, the colder the region, and vice versa.

While usually the urban areas are a bit more protected and a few degrees warmer in wintertime, the scorching summer sun can be just as damaging as the freezing winter. The Heat Zone Map categorizes places based on the number of days the mercury rises to 86°F (30°C). Zone 1 includes areas where the temperature climbs to 86°F (30°C) one day a year or less, while zone 12 marks places where the temperature hovers around 86°F (30°C) or higher for more than 210 days.

Identifying your subzone will help you make more precise decisions while selecting fruit trees for your garden. Start by finding your overarching zone then narrow down your search with your zip code to identify your region's subzone. Knowing your zone helps you save time and money in the long run by avoiding plants destined to fail in your area. You can guarantee success by selecting fruit trees suited to your region.

Chill Hours

Another important point to consider while choosing what to grow is the number of chill hours. Most deciduous trees undergo a period of dormancy during winter. The chilling requirement of a fruit tree refers to the minimum duration of cold weather necessary to bring a fruit-bearing tree out of dormancy. Typically measured in chill hours, various methods exist to calculate this requirement, all involving the accumulation of time spent at specific temperatures during the winter season.

If a tree fits your gardening zone but your location does not fulfill its chill hour requirements, then you may witness less fruit production. Temperate fruit trees need anywhere between 100 to 1,400 chill hours to bear fruit in the upcoming season. Chill hours are usually a matter of concern for regions in USDA zones 9b and 10. These include mostly southern and coastal areas, which have average chill hours of 100 to 600 per year. If you reside in these locations, you should keep an eye on the chill requirements of the fruits you plan to grow. Fruits that require low chill hours include persimmons, almonds, olives, pomegranates, berries, and some varieties of apples, apricots, peaches, pears, and plums.

If a tree doesn't get enough chill hours during the winter, the flower buds may not bloom during spring or open unevenly. Moreover, leaf growth might also be delayed. Similarly, a tree with low chill hours in a high-chill area may flower too early, so late winter frosts may damage the fruit.

Spoilt for Choice: Selecting Fruit Tree Varieties

Imagine a tree that fits in your yard just right. Its canopy is just the right size, creating a sanctuary for the shade-loving plants at its base without casting a shadow on your vegetable patch. It can easily withstand weather fluctuations in your area while bearing delicious fruit impossible to find in grocery stores near you.

The first rule of edible gardening is to plant what you like to eat. The same principle applies to fruit trees. Growing up at my grandparents' farm in the valley, I have fond memories of eating meltingly delicious, ripe apricots. Fast forward a few years, and finding a decent apricot at the local market where I live seemed nearly impossible! Most fruit tree owners have their own childhood memories of a favorite fruit—a peach that grew over their neighbor's fence, or grapes from their great uncle's home garden. Similarly, canners and bakers choose fruits that best fit their purposes.

If you've got your heart set on growing a particular fruit tree, don't go out to buy it just yet. As mentioned above, how well your fruit tree performs in your area depends on various factors. High and low temperatures during different seasons, soil quality, amount of frost, and the length of the growing season all contribute toward the success of your orchard.

Some trees might not bear fruit during adverse conditions or might produce fruit so rarely they're not worth the trouble. Some trees wither while others die outright. Others may produce low-quality fruit that doesn't match your expectations. All this can be avoided by selecting fruit tree varieties guaranteed to thrive in your location. For example, peaches grown in areas with cool summers often lack flavor. You can put your time and energy to better use by accepting the realities of climate limitations and selecting varieties that are bound to flourish.

Keeping the size and climate restrictions of your area in mind, there are thousands of fruit varieties for you to choose from. Blenheim apricots and Santa Rosa plums are popular candidates for backyard orchards due to their rich flavor and reliable behavior. Sweet, juicy, crunchy Fuji apples grow well in hot climates like the Central Valley in California where most apple varieties falter. They may even thrive in cooler climates like the East Bay if the growing season is long enough and they get sufficient heat during late summer. Cox's Orange Pippin apples are great candidates for eating fresh, just as Yellow Newton Pippins are for pies. Choosing dwarf varieties and planting them close together will leave you with just enough space to experiment. For example, in the case of apples, you can try growing varieties such as Yellow Bellflower, Hudson's Golden Gem, or Wickson Crab.

Talking to local orchard owners, nurseries, and people at the farmers' markets will give you the best indication of which fruits grow best in your area. Make sure to consider other characteristics of the trees you choose in addition to taste and flavor. For instance, Gravenstein apples may taste wonderful but have a short shelf life. Similarly, the Emerald Beaut plum needs a pollenizer and has an unappealing appearance.

Another important point to keep in mind while going through the selection process is to remember that the trees will take some time to bear fruit. Chart 3 will give you an idea of how long it takes for different trees to bear fruit, so you can choose accordingly. Remember that the years in this chart are counted after a tree is transplanted to the growing site. Keep in mind that most trees that you buy may already be one or two years old. Chart 3 lists the estimated yield of different fruit trees, so you can prepare for storage.

Chart 3: Years to bear fruit of different trees

Fruit Trees	Years to Fruit
Apple Trees	2-5 years
Avocado Trees	3-4 years
Apricot Trees	2-5 years
Banana Plants	2-3 years
Cherry Trees (sour)	3-5 years
Cherry Trees (sweet)	4-7 years
Citrus Trees	1-3 years
Fig Trees	1-3 years
Jujube Trees	2-5 years
Mulberry Trees	2-3 years
Nectarine Trees	2-4 years
Olive Trees	2-4 years
Pawpaw Trees	2-7 years
Peach Trees	2-4 years

Pear Trees	4-7 years
Persimmon Trees	3-4 years
Plum Trees	3-6 years
Pomegranate Trees	2-3 years

Chart 4: Estimated yield of fruit trees

Fruit Trees	Estimated Yield
Apple Trees	Miniature: 1/4–1 bushel Dwarf: 1–4 bushels Semi-Dwarf: 5–10 bushels Standard: 10–20 bushels
Apricot	Dwarf: 1–3 bushels Standard: 3–6 bushels
Cherry	Sour Varieties Dwarf: 15–20 quarts Semi-Dwarf: 20–60 quarts Sweet Varieties Dwarf: 15–20 quarts Semi-Dwarf: 30–50 quarts Standard: 60–75 quarts (~3 bushels)
Nectarine	Dwarf: 2–3 bushels Standard: 3–5 bushels
Peach	Dwarf: 1–3 bushels Standard: 3–6 bushels
Pear	Asian Varieties Dwarf: 2–3 bushels Standard: 4–6 bushels

	European Varieties Dwarf: 1–3 bushels Standard: 3–6 bushels
Plum	Japanese Varieties Dwarf: 1/2–2 bushel Standard: 2–4 bushel European Varieties Dwarf: 1–2 bushel Standard: 3–6 bushels

Bushel: a measure of capacity equal to 64 US pints / 8 gallons / appr 35-36 liters.

Tools, Equipment, and Resources

There are various tools available for gardening, each serving different purposes. You can either invest in high-quality ones that will serve you well every time, or opt for cheaper alternatives that may leave you disappointed after a few uses. If you're on a budget and not tending to many plants, you might decide to spend less; however, make an effort to maintain them properly, keeping the blades sharp, joints oiled, and everything clean to ensure they function properly in the long run.

Good tools not only perform better, producing cleaner cuts that are less likely to invite disease, but they also enhance the gardening experience, turning it into a pleasure rather than a chore. Your inventory will vary depending on what you choose to grow. Here are some essential items you should have with you to look after your orchard:

1. **Secateurs:** These are like heavy-duty mini garden shears and are indispensable for various plant-cutting tasks. They can easily cut through branches up to 1 cm thick. Felco secateurs are widely regarded as the best.

2. **Loppers:** These are essentially heavy-duty secateurs with long handles, often extendable, allowing you to prune hard-to-reach

areas with extra reach and leverage. Some loppers have a ratcheting action, making it easier to prune thicker branches.

3. **Penknife:** While there are specialized garden knives available for specific tasks like grafting and pruning, it's sufficient to keep a well-made penknife in your pocket for general use. Ensure it is always sharp. It can be handy for tidying up minor damage, making precise cuts, taking cuttings, and cutting string.

4. **Pruning saw:** For cutting thick branches, a pruning saw is necessary. These curved mini-saws are tapered to enable pruning in tight spaces and can have single or double-edged blades. Invest in a high-quality pruning saw that can withstand the force required for cutting. You may not need one immediately unless you have mature plants that require pruning.

5. **Fork:** The workhorse for soil turning and plant lifting, a fork is excellent for turning compost and incorporating compost or manure into the soil. Investing in a good-quality fork is wise.

6. **Spade:** Used for digging, cutting straight edges, and turning fine compost that is difficult to handle with a fork.

7. **Trowel and hand fork:** These basic tools are ideal for small-scale digging, soil turning, and weeding in tight spaces.

In addition to these, a wheelbarrow, a watering can, and two buckets or trugs may also come in handy. These will prove useful for various tasks, particularly during planting time. Other items to consider include a step ladder, shredder, a hoe, a rake, a water butt, rubber-ended mallet for stakes, tree ties, tree guards against rabbits and deer, and a sharpening stone to keep your blades sharp.

Maintenance Tips

Simply owning top-quality tools is not enough; you must also maintain them properly to ensure they remain in excellent condition. Here are some valuable tips on how to effectively service your shovels and pruners.

Tip 1: After using steel garden tools, take the time to clean off any soil or debris using a wire brush. Once cleaned, wipe them down with an oil rag. Accumulated soil and rust can add unnecessary weight and diminish the tools' effectiveness.

Tip 2: To rejuvenate wooden-handled tools, apply paste wax (readily available at hardware stores) every few years. This practice helps condition the wood, keeping it in optimal shape.

Tip 3: Pay close attention to your pruners. Regularly clean them, ensuring they are free from sap. Lubricate them with pruner grease, which you can find at garden centers or online. Store your pruners in a leather sheath to protect the blade and maintain its sharpness.

The Takeaway

Let's round up everything we've learned so far. Setting up a backyard orchard requires careful thought and meticulous planning. By evaluating your place, and noting sunlight patterns, wind intensity, and soil quality, you can find the best trees for your orchard that require minimal care to thrive. There are thousands of varieties for you to choose from to fulfill your dreams of growing a particular fruit in your home garden. Investing in high-quality tools and maintaining them over time allows you to take better care of your fruit trees.

Once you've made a mental map, it's time to move on to building the blueprint for your backyard garden. So get a pen and paper ready, because in Chapter 2 we'll be looking at building an effective garden layout as well as the perfect soil for growing a successful fruit garden.

CHAPTER 2

Building Your Orchard Blueprint

Imagine rows of vast Bramley apple trees stretching across rolling pastures, their branches heavy with fruit—an orchard nestled within the grounds of an old country estate, carefully tended by generations of skilled gardeners to provide fresh fruit for the house. Such grand orchards might make you feel envious. The small patch of land you have to work with might feel inadequate or insufficient. It's important to realize that orchards can thrive in smaller spaces too. All that's required is a set of smart decisions. The process of designing an orchard applies to everyone, whether you're planting just a few trees or several hundred.

When it comes to planting trees in an orchard, there's no one-size-fits-all approach. The positioning of trees depends on the unique characteristics of each site, resulting in variations from place to place. Traditionally, orchards were organized in a grid formation, with rows of trees running from north to south. This setup aimed to maximize sun exposure for every tree. But nowadays, there's room for creativity and personal preference. Some orchard owners prefer a more organic and curved arrangement, adding a touch of artistic flair to their groves. Urban sites with plenty of sunlight and good soil can still adopt the grid pattern if desired, but flexibility is key.

Designing an Efficient and Productive Garden Layout

In certain situations, orchard trees may be grouped together in clusters, taking advantage of suitable patches of land. This is often seen in estates that have multiple grassy areas. The important thing is to ensure that each tree is positioned in a spot that receives enough sunlight, has adequate soil depth, proper drainage, and isn't cramped too close to other trees or large shrubs.

Giving fruit trees ample space to grow without competing with each other is essential. For example, for semi-dwarfing tree varieties like MM106, it's recommended to space them about 5 meters apart. For M26, the distance should be around 3.5 to 4 meters. This spacing not only promotes healthy growth but also allows sufficient light to reach the ground, opening up possibilities for planting companion species like herbs and soft fruit in the future.

Orchard Layout and Design Principles

When planting trees, it's crucial to consider their eventual size. For instance, if you're planting next to a towering oak that's already 4 meters tall, keep in mind that it will continue to grow both taller and wider. So, planting just 5 meters away might not provide enough space in the long run. It's wise to think ahead and give trees the room they need to thrive.

Now, let's circle back to Chapter 1 and talk about two significant factors that can make or break an orchard: cold-air drainage and soil quality. To create an ideal orchard site, aim for an elevated location on the upper side of a gradual slope, ideally between four to percent. This helps ensure proper cold-air drainage, as low-lying areas are more prone to frost damage during calm, clear nights. On the flip side, hilltops or ridges can expose trees to harsh winds or extreme cold.

When it comes to soil, orchards flourish in deep, well-drained, and aerated loam. It's crucial to conduct thorough soil appraisals well in advance of planting. Start by finding a soil map and digging test holes to examine the soil profile. Soil maps provide valuable information about its texture, parent material, fertility levels, erosion risks, and water-holding capacity. Test holes help identify any issues like impervious layers or water-related problems. By checking the test holes during rainy periods, you can gather vital information about the soil water table.

During this assessment, be sure to collect samples of the topsoil and subsoil for analysis. These samples help determine important factors like pH levels, nutrient imbalances, and organic matter content. Additionally, consider other site-specific factors such as water accessibility for irrigation and spraying, the presence of weed reservoirs that could harbor plant viruses, and the potential risks of hailstorms or other weather-related disasters.

Evaluating the above factors allows you to select the perfect orchard site that optimizes cold-air drainage, boasts high-quality soil, and lays the groundwork for a successful and profitable orchard operation.

The Plan: The Magic Formula

The success of your orchard hinges on devising a solid plan before you start planting. Before committing yourself to a certain layout, you should take into account various factors like the space available, the equipment on hand, and your available time, and choose varieties, rootstocks, and planting densities accordingly. The density of trees in an orchard has a significant impact on its efficiency. Higher density orchards, with 500 or more trees per acre on dwarf rootstocks, require more attention from growers, including timely tree training, pruning, and water management.

The goal is to find the right balance between maximizing the bearing capacity per acre and avoiding overcrowding. Trees should be spaced so that they touch at maturity without becoming cramped. Various factors like variety vigor, rootstock size control, climate, soil fertility, growing season length, available water, and light intensity influence the mature size of the trees.

In modern orchards, the trend is toward higher-density plantings of small trees. Semi-dwarf orchards typically have densities ranging from 123 to 311 trees per acre (1 acre = appr. 4045 m^2), while dwarf orchards can reach densities of 388 to 777 trees per acre, sometimes with spacings as tight as 2' x 10'. High-density orchards now exceed 500 trees per acre and can even go beyond 1000 trees with multi-row systems. Here's an easy formula to estimate the number of trees per acre on your land:

Trees/Acre = 43,560/L*W

L = spacing between trees in feet for direction 1

W = spacing between trees in feet for direction 2

Considering these factors and making informed choices regarding rootstocks, scion varieties, and planting density, orchard planners can optimize their operations for success.

Maximizing Sunlight Penetration

An important factor to keep in mind while designing the layout is how light is intercepted and distributed within the canopy, particularly to the flowers and fruit. If you opt for branched trees on dwarfing rootstocks, you can expect early crops, which is fantastic.

Now, here's an interesting tip: trees grown in north-south rows tend to have better light conditions compared to those grown in east-west rows. So, when planning your orchard layout, keep this in mind. You can further enhance light interception by reducing the distance between rows and increasing the height of the trees. As a general rule, aim for a tree height that is half the row spacing plus an additional three feet. This will help optimize production per acre.

To ensure your orchard plan is successful, it's wise to order your trees two to three years ahead of planting. This allows you to obtain the best scion/rootstock combinations that suit your specific needs. Look for virus-tested trees with healthy root systems to give your orchard a strong start and set the foundation for sustainable production. If you're planning an intensive system, having well-feathered trees is desirable for early cropping.

Additionally, if you require windbreak trees or pollinizers, it's best to order them early as well. Studies suggest that alders, willows, or other deciduous species that leaf out early and retain leaves until after harvest make excellent windbreak trees. And don't forget to seek local advice on the best pollinizers, as fruit tree bloom periods can vary from region to region.

Soil: Your Roadmap to Success

Ensuring the right balance of reserve food and soil elements for your trees is crucial for fruitful success. If your tree is well fed but growing in the wrong soil, you might end up with a disappointing harvest of small, lackluster fruits or even no fruits at all. This can occur if the tree has gone into overdrive, trying to produce too much and causing premature fruit drop. It can also happen if the tree has suffered from leaf depletion due to stress, weather, pests, or diseases. Identifying and addressing the underlying issue will help resolve the problem.

Soil pH

Picture a scale from 1 to 14, where 7 is the neutral sweet spot. Anything below 7 is on the acidic side, while anything above is considered more alkaline. Fruit trees are generally content in the pH range of 6 to 6.5, but they can tolerate a slightly higher or lower pH without throwing a fit. Almond trees, however, prefer a pH range of 7 to 7.5, with their optimal zone sitting around 5. So, optimizing your soil pH is definitely worth the effort.

Now, let's talk about some high-maintenance plants, such as blueberries, and almonds. They have specific pH preferences, and straying too far from their desired range won't bode well for their growth. It's like trying to make a coffee lover settle for tea—they won't be thrilled. And here's a no-brainer: very few plants can handle the extreme ends of the pH scale.

So, how can you uncover the pH secrets of your soil? Well, you have a couple of options. You can go for a soil test conducted by a university or private lab. Or you can simply use a home test kit. Adjusting soil pH is like fine-tuning an instrument. To increase pH and make it more alkaline, you can add lime. If you want to lower the pH, sulfur or a sulfur-containing fertilizer is your trusty tool.

Remember, soil pH is like a harmonious melody for your plants. Striving for the right pH balance is essential for their well-being, just like finding the perfect rhythm. It's a fun journey that brings out the scientist in you!

Texture

Soil texture refers to the size of the soil particles. Think of it like different types of soil personalities. We've got sandy soil, which has these larger particles that just fall apart when you squeeze them. They can't hold themselves together. Then there's loam soil, with slightly smaller particles. When you give it a good squeeze, it takes a few minutes before it falls apart. And finally, we've got clay soil. This one is made up of tiny particles that hold their shape no matter what.

But here's the interesting part. Most soils out there are a mix of these types, so you might have a mixture of sandy loam or clay loam. And depending on where you are, certain types of soil are more common. You'll find clay soil in some regions, sandy soil on hilltops, and loam soil down in the lowlands near rivers.

Different soils have different superpowers when it comes to water. Sandy soil is like a speedster, draining water real quick. Loam soil is more of a moderate drinker, taking its time to let the water seep through. And clay soil? It's the water hoarder of the group, holding onto that moisture for longer periods. So, if you've got fruit trees growing on a sandy hill, they might be pretty thirsty and need more water. But if they're rooted in clay soil, they might get more water than they need.

When it comes to growing trees, loam soil is the golden ticket. It's the all-around champ for garden crops and fruit trees. However, with a little TLC, you can make plants grow in any soil texture. It's just that some soils make it easier for plant roots to spread their wings, or should I say, their roots. Sandy soil is like an open invitation for roots to explore, while clay soil can be a bit restrictive, keeping those roots on a tight leash.

Now, I won't sugarcoat it. Growing fruit trees in clay soil can be a bit of a challenge. But don't worry, we've got some tricks up our sleeves. Adding things like compost and mulches to the mix can work wonders. They help improve the drainage and give those roots a bit more breathing room. So even in clay soil, we can turn things around and create a cozy home for those fruit trees. It just takes a little extra effort and some organic magic.

Soil Fertility

Researchers have identified more than 16 essential mineral elements that are necessary for the growth of tree fruits. The specific quantity required varies for each element. Generally, our soils contain sufficient amounts of these essential elements for fruit trees. However, there are five minerals—nitrogen, phosphorus, potassium, calcium, and boron—that deserve closer attention in orchards due to the potential for shortages to occur. It is important to monitor and manage these minerals carefully to ensure optimal growth and development of fruit trees. We'll discuss these in more detail in Chapter 3.

The Takeaway

Considering the ultimate size of mature trees, sunlight penetration, airflow, and cold drainage allows you to devise the perfect orchard layout. You can avoid potential problems in your backyard fruit garden by carefully analyzing your space and choosing trees accordingly. By adjusting the soil pH, texture, and nutrient content according to your plants' needs, you can provide them with a solid foundation to build on, setting them off to a strong start.

CHAPTER 3

Planting and Establishing Fruit Trees

Now that you've done all the planning, it's time to head over to your local gardening center or nursery and bring the trees home. This may seem like a simple task of pick up and go, but ending up with an unhealthy tree could cost you a fortune. Keep in mind that choosing a higher quality nursery increases your chances of going home with healthy trees. Always choose reputable garden centers or nurseries with a proven track record of providing healthy trees.

Selecting Healthy Fruit Tree Stocks and Rootstocks

By now you may have prepared a list of fruit tree varieties that you want to grow on your property. However, finding a healthy tree may prove tricky. To the untrained eye, all trees may look the same. Meanwhile, arborists spend years learning the distinguishing characteristics of numerous tree varieties. Tree enthusiasts can easily spot a healthy tree, free from pests and disease, that is bound to thrive in your orchard with minimal care.

Tree Vocabulary

Before you head off to the nursery, it's best to brush up on your tree vocabulary. By learning a few key terms, you can avoid feeling lost, read tree tags, and make the best decisions. Here are some basic terms you should know:

- **Family:** A group of trees that closely resemble each other in appearance.
- **Genus:** A division within the same family wherein the trees share multiple similar traits.
- **Species:** A subdivision of genus, which further narrows down the trees grouped together.
- **Variety:** A division of the species into a smaller group with defining characteristics.
- **Hybrid:** A group of cross-bred trees that are not found naturally.
- **Clones:** Trees propagated by using cuttings from the parent plant.
- **Caliper:** The diameter of the tree's trunk.
- **Tree Leader:** The dominant vertical stem at the top of the tree trunk.

Finding a Healthy Tree

At this point, you may have a clear idea about the trees you want and where you want to plant them. This means you'll have the answers ready to the first questions the nursery staff might ask when you arrive. Narrowing down your list to the species level will make the job even easier. Once you have all that sorted, it's time to carefully inspect the tree. Here are a few identifying traits of healthy trees:

- No brown leaves curling at the tips indicating water deficiency
- Minimal or no scarring on the trunk and branches
- No blotches or holes indicating insect infestation
- Few dead branches and twigs
- A well-developed top leader
- Trunks that narrow uniformly

- Branches that are well-distributed and spaced 8 to 12 inches apart

While the above attributes can give you a general idea about the tree's structural health, it's what lies underground that matters the most. The roots hold the answer to any questions you might have regarding the health of the tree. While structural defects can be easily corrected, compromised root systems can signal deeper problems.

Roots: The Secret to Healthy Trees

The complex network of roots not only anchors the trees but also ensures the absorption of nutrients and water. Here are some signs that should ring alarm bells if you detect them on your trees' roots:**Root Ball Dimensions:** The size of the root ball should be in proportion to the tree height. It should neither be larger nor smaller than the tree trunk.

1. **Root Collar:** This is the mass of roots that meets the trunk base above ground level. It must not be more than an inch above or below the earth. If the root collar is too exposed, then it's a sign of poor tree health.

2. **Circling Roots:** These occur when the tree has overgrown its container. With nowhere to go, the roots begin circling the pot. Such trees may require root pruning before being transplanted.

3. **Stem-girdling Roots:** Such roots are formed when they're cut and begin growing perpendicular. They may cause indentations on the trunk, inviting a number of diseases.

4. **Root Bound Trees:** While such trees aren't necessarily unhealthy, they may indicate lack of professional attention and may point toward other health problems lurking underneath.

You can accurately estimate root strength by using the flex test. Hold the tree trunk with one hand while applying gentle pressure on the container or the root ball with the other. If the root ball stays firm and the trunk bends or flexes, it's a good sign. But if the roots flex and the trunk remains rigid then you might want to look for another.

Rootstock

Fruit trees are not commonly grown from seeds because when they are, the fruit usually doesn't measure up to the grower's expectations. Moreover, left to their own devices, fruit trees can grow massive, becoming difficult for gardeners to manage.

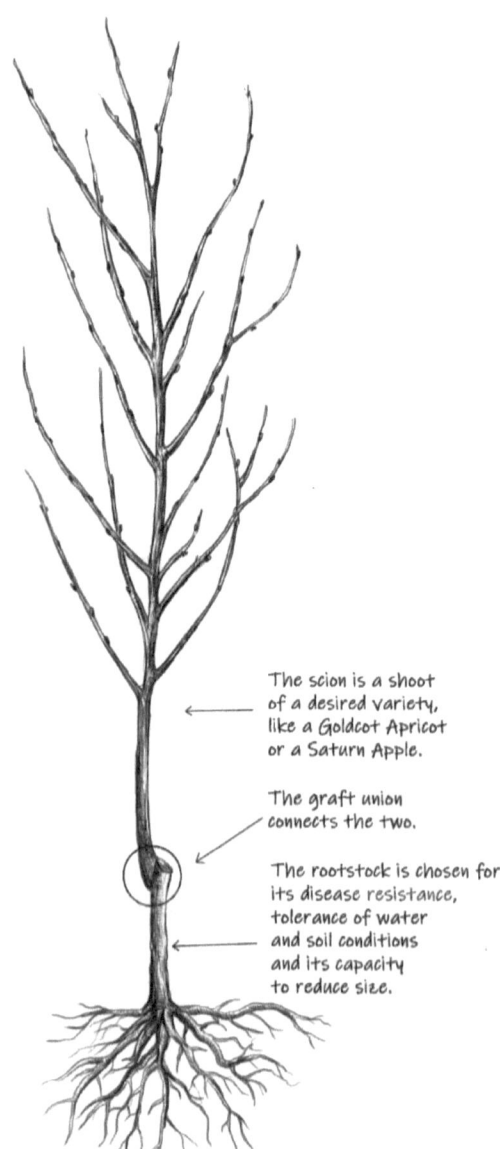

Figure 3: A grafted tree and its parts

This is why most fruit trees are cross pollinated. The resulting tree shares some DNA with its mother tree and some with its father tree. Seeds produced by such trees have unique genetic make-up, and eventually grow into trees that produce fruit unlike the fruit of the parent trees.

Grafted fruit trees have two parts: the scion, the part of the tree above the ground, and the rootstock, the bottom portion of the trunk consisting of the roots. A scion is grafted onto a rootstock of a related tree to create varieties that have a more manageable size and produce the best quality fruit. Figure 3 and 4 illustrate the anatomy of new and of a few year old grafted fruit tree.

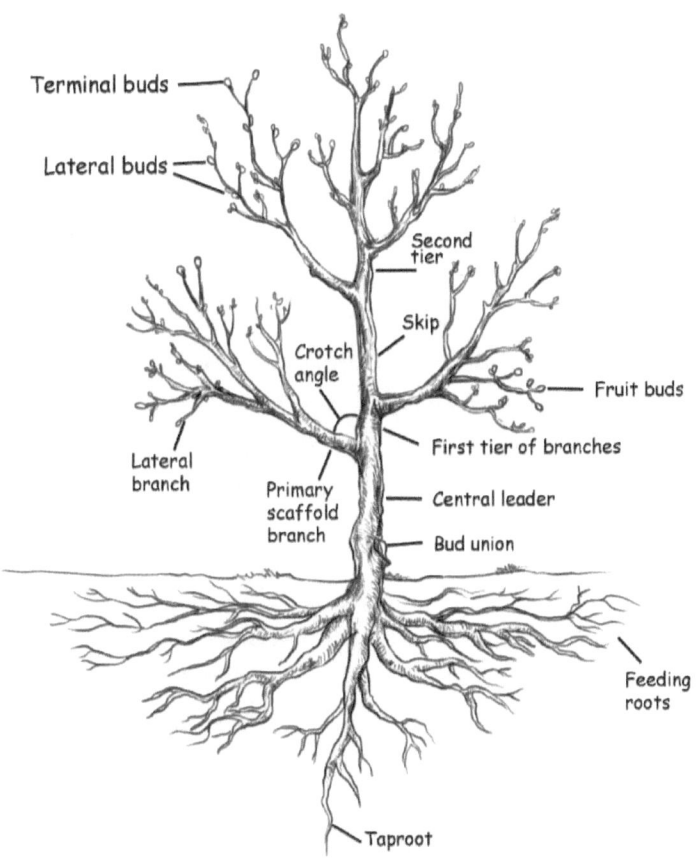

Figure 4: The anatomy of a few-year-old grafted fruit tree.

When you go out to buy a fruit tree, check out the label and you'll find the rootstock it's grafted on. Some benefits of using rootstocks include that they:

1. Add desirable traits to the plant such as pest and disease resistance, cold hardiness, increased fruit production, and smaller tree size.

2. Create trees that bear fruit quickly rather than taking three to eight years.

3. Produce dwarf or semi-dwarf varieties that are easier to grow, encouraging gardeners to plant more trees per acre and achieve a higher fruit yield.

Let's look at the three different categories of root stock and which one you should choose for your orchard:

Standard

Trees that can grow up to 25 feet or more fit in this category. Regular pruning can limit the size of these trees to 26 x 20 feet with a height of 24 feet. In contrast to dwarf varieties, standards tend to live longer and produce more fruit. Being late bloomers, they take anywhere from five to eight years to bear fruit and can be difficult to prune.

Dwarf

Small trees for small spaces, their compact size makes them easy to prune and harvest. They take three to five years to begin fruiting and have limited root networks benefiting from supplemental irrigation during dry spells.

Semi-Dwarf

Lying somewhere between standard and dwarf varieties, these trees range anywhere between 10 to 16 ft tall. Timely pruning can keep them in shape. The fruits are the same size as standard trees while fruit bearing generally begins three to five years after planting.

Take Your Pick: Rootballed, Containerized, or Bare Root

Most plants and trees that you'll find at the nursery will be in containers, usually black plastic pots packed with compost. While most plants spend their entire lives, others are grown in the ground and shifted to pots before being put up for sale (containerized). On the other hand, bare root trees remain in the ground for their entire lifetime. They usually turn up for sale after entering dormancy in the winter months when they're dug up and sold without a pot or soil.

Meanwhile, rootballed plants are grown in the ground, dug up, and sold with a ball of soil protecting the delicate roots. The mass of root and soil is wrapped in a hessian square to provide the necessary structural support. This technique is usually applied on plants that don't transplant well through the bare root method because they either don't go entirely dormant or because they have extremely fragile root structure.

Traditionally, bare root trees and plants dominated the market in the '40s and '50s before plastic pots took over. The biggest drawback of opting for bare root is limited window for planting them. For instance, if you intend to plant in April or May, you'll wait until the beginning of next season to receive them. However, the advantages greatly outnumber the minor inconvenience of waiting. You have a wide variety of trees of different sizes to choose from with strong root systems. It's best to plant during the winter months, allowing the new trees to accustom themselves to their new location before sprouting blooms and foliage.

Each method mentioned above has its own pros and cons. Containerized trees tend to be the most convenient and are readily available throughout the year. If you don't have the planting site ready, you can keep them in pots for weeks or even months after bringing them home. However, you'll have a smaller variety, size, and rootstock to choose from and the prices will be higher than bare root trees. Then there is the issue of single-use plastic pots that'll most likely end up in landfills.

As for bare root trees, unpacking and planting must be done within three to four days after arrival. Old gardening books might mention November or December as the ideal time for planting because the soil is relatively warm and retains sufficient moisture from autumn rains. However, you can plant anytime during the winter, as long as you can push a spade into the ground. Some frost or a thin covering of snow usually isn't a problem. The only time planting isn't an option is when the ground is frozen solid or the soil is waterlogged. In this scenario, digging the bare roots into a heap of compost or loose soil and waiting for the ground to thaw is your best bet.

Timing is Everything: Answering the When, Where and How

Let's get into the nitty gritty of when, where, and how to plant the trees once they've arrived at your property.

When to Plant

- In mild climates, planting fruit bushes and trees from November onward gives the roots a few extra weeks to establish. Planting during this time of the year usually isn't a problem for areas in the South and Pacific Northwest.

- In cold regions, the ideal time for planting bare-rooted trees is toward the end of winter or the beginning of spring when the ground is no longer frozen.

- If the ground outside isn't ready, you can pack bare root trees in moist earth and wait for a few days until conditions are more favorable. Ideally, bare root trees must be planted after arrival.

- If you miss the ideal time for planting trees, it's best to opt for containerized trees. The roots of container-grown trees are already established and ready to absorb moisture and nutrients during warmer weather.

Where to Plant

- Choose an area that meets the tree's sunlight requirements.
- Avoid areas prone to flooding, or located on higher ground where the soil can dry out quickly.
- Create a sheltered environment for the trees by planting near a fence or a wall to block strong winds.
- Avoid planting near your house's roof, which can dump a heap of snow on the unsuspecting tree, breaking branches.
- Keep an eye on other plants in the tree's surroundings. The trees are exceptionally good at absorbing nutrients and water, depriving other plants of their essential requirements.

How to Plant

- Grab a spade and dig a square hole that's about three feet wide. The square shape encourages root growth into the surrounding ground better than a round one.
- Fill the hole with a few inches of compost, mixing it with the soil underneath with a garden fork.
- Use the soil you removed from the ground, mix it with the remaining compost and put aside.
- Search the tree's trunk for a slightly dark watermark. This is where the soil level was at where the tree grew before.
- Put the bare-rooted tree in the center and use a cane to ensure the soil reaches the mark on the trunk. Make sure the joint of the grafted tree remains above the ground.
- Take the tree out and place a thick wooden stake a few inches away from the center in the hole. Hammer it firmly into place on the side where strong winds usually blow over your property.

- Replace the tree in the hole, close to the stake, and begin shoveling soil and compost mix you prepared earlier. This process is known as backfilling.

- Press the soil gently with your boots as you go along. When you're halfway done, lift the tree up by grabbing the trunk then let go, allowing it to sink again. This will make sure there aren't any empty spaces around the roots.

- Tie the trunk with the stake when you're done, making sure to leave enough room for tree growth while providing the necessary support. You can also add a protective tube around the tree to ward off small animals and scatter seaweed meal fertilizer at the base.

- Cover the ground with biodegradable hemp mat to prevent weed growth.

- Water the soil deeply so the roots don't dry out and the soil settles around them.

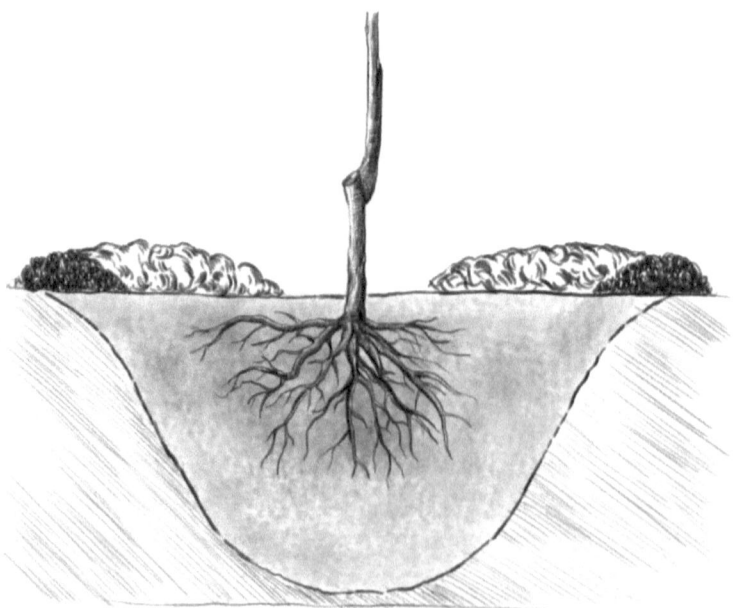

Figure 5: The correct placement of the tree in the hole.

Staking: Protect Your Young Trees

For the first two years, your tree will require staking to keep it straight. This will prevent strong gusts of wind from knocking the tree over when it's young and uprooting it. Stakes are particularly important for young trees because they lack proper root systems that anchor them to the ground. Without the necessary support, the trees may develop a 'crowbar hole.' If the wind causes the newly planted tree to rock back and forth too much, the friction can create a widening gap between the trunk and the hole. A dwarf tree with shallow anchorage or bare root trees are usually prone to developing this condition.

While staking is usually necessary, it can disrupt growth of the trunk and root system if performed on the wrong tree. Here are some scenarios in which staking is a prerequisite:

- Planting bare root trees
- Planting trees unable to stand on their own
- Planting in an area prone to seasonal flooding
- Planting in an extremely windy site
- Planting a tree with an extremely small root ball

Materials that you should use to install the stakes should allow the trunk to move naturally while providing sufficient support. These can include elastic straps, strips of cotton fabric, bicycle tubes, nylon stockings, and slings that you may find in garden centers. It's advisable to use wide straps which will provide flexible support while causing injury to the tree. Make a figure eight with the strap and tie loosely to the stake. Take a look at the Figure 6 below to get a better idea about using slings with stakes.

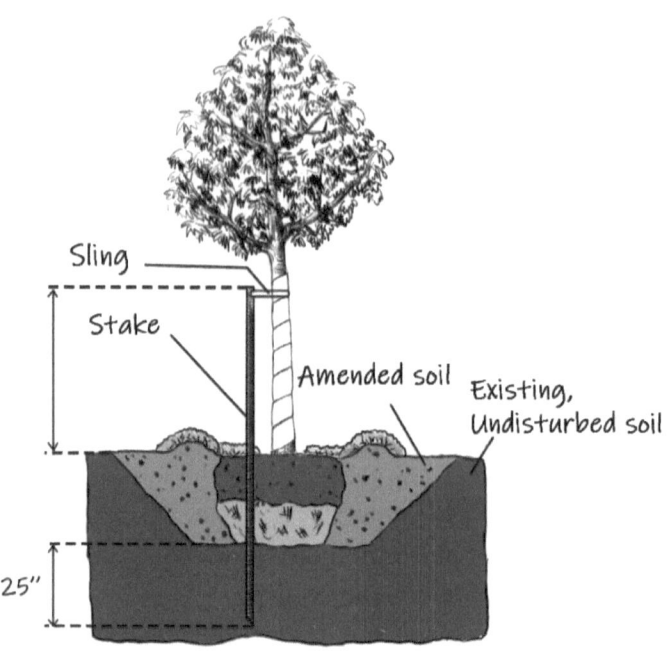

Figure 6: Planting a tree using stakes and sling.

Now that we've discussed the materials you'll need, let's take a look at the different methods of staking.

Single Stake

- Use this method if the tree's trunk is smaller than 5 cm in diameter.
- Add the stake after placing the tree in the hole. Take care to avoid the root ball and install on the side that receives the most wind.
- Bury the stake at least 60 cm in the ground. The part of the stake above the ground should not exceed two-thirds of the trunk.
- Attach a strap, if necessary, to the end of the stake.

Two or Three Stakes

- Use two to three stakes if the diameter of the tree trunk is 5 to 10 cm.
- Install the stakes on both sides of the tree after placing it in the hole. If you're using three stakes, place them in the shape of a triangle.
- Bury the stakes up to 60 cm in the soil. The part above the ground shouldn't reach more than two-thirds up the trunk.
- Attach the strap at the end of one stake.

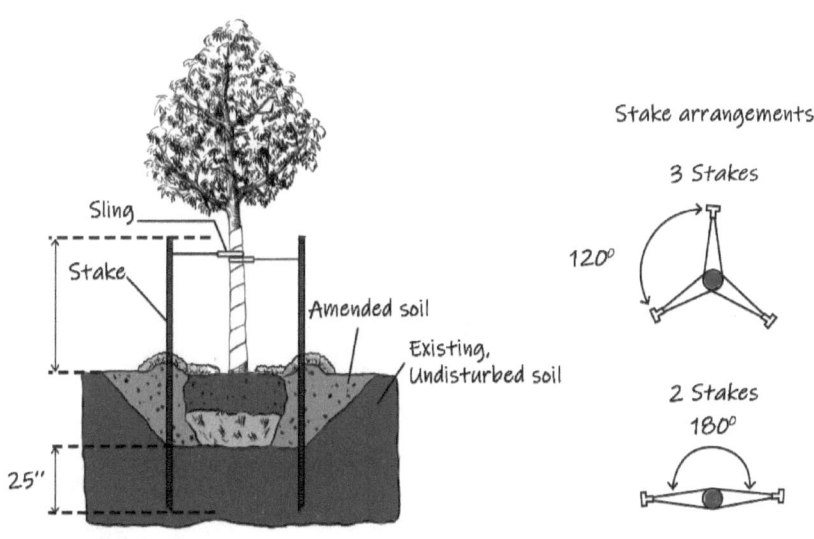

Figure 7: Using two and three stakes to plant trees

Staking with Guy Wires

- Use guy wires if the tree's trunk is more than 10 cm in diameter.
- Fasten three cables with three other cables using turnbuckles. These are known as guy wires.
- Use wooden stakes or galvanized steel for anchoring.

- Take three inch-wide elastic straps and fasten the guy wires to the trunk. This process will be much easier with grommets.
- Place the anchors in the soil after planting the tree. Place them at a 30-degree angle away from the planting hole in a triangle.
- Fasten the guy wires at the base.
- Fix the straps on the trunk.
- Pass the guy wires through the eyelets and stretch them at a 45-degree angle from the tree.
- Make sure the wires don't touch the trunk.
- Inspect the tree regularly for any signs of damage.

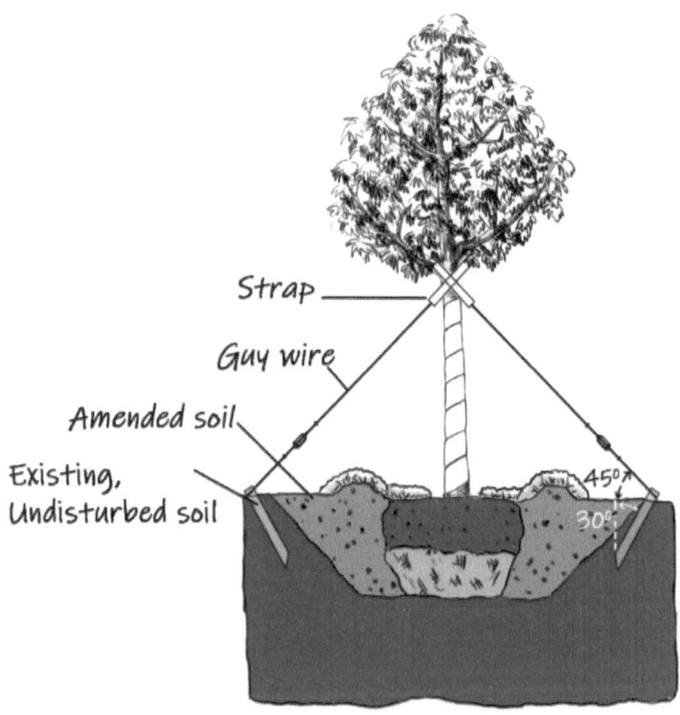

Figure 8: Using guy wires to stake a tree

Remember that staking is a temporary solution. The stakes should be removed as soon as possible to avoid damaging the tree, encouraging the development of a strong trunk and root system. Usually, stakes are taken out after the first year. However, you may have to wait up to two years to remove them from larger trees. If you're unsure, grab the trunk and give it a little shake to check if the root ball is loose. If it stays firm, the tree no longer requires staking.

Irrigation Strategies

The amount of water that a fruit tree needs depends on its size, day length, and the weather, including factors such as temperature, humidity, and wind. Inadequate watering can result in smaller fruits and stunted growth. Extreme drought can lead to a poor harvest, causing the fruits to burn, shrivel up, and fall, in addition to leaf dropping. However, established trees with deeper roots tend to benefit from infrequent watering. Such trees can tolerate getting watered every three to four weeks from June to August. Meanwhile, young trees require watering every ten days or after every two weeks.

Generally, trees require two gallons of water per day one to two years after planting, while mature trees may need up to fifty gallons on hot summer days. Watering the plants slowly will ensure the soil absorbs all the moisture. Young trees tend to be more susceptible to water stress than established ones. And while you may have the impression citrus trees are drought resistant, their shallow roots make them prone to water stress (von Rosenberg, 2015). So, how can you make sure you water the trees in your orchard just right? Here are some important points to help you get the hang of your fruit tree's watering needs:

1. Invest in a great irrigation system that ensures deep watering.
2. Apply a generous layer of mulch around the trees to help the soil retain moisture.
3. Plant dwarf or semi-dwarf varieties that are easier to manage.
4. Prune hard, cutting the tree back by about one-third, especially during dormancy.
5. Understand each tree's watering requirement and water according. Figs, almonds, and olives are the most drought-

resistant, while peaches, citrus, and nectarines are the least drought-resistant.

6. Make sure the soil is healthy with plenty of organic matter to lock in the moisture.

Orchard Irrigation: Finding What Suits You Best?

Irrigation methods commonly used by gardeners include soaker hoses, drip irrigation, and sprinklers. So which method is the best one? The answer, unsurprisingly, is that it depends. Various factors go into choosing the right irrigation system for your garden. Figure 9 depicts the different irrigation systems (drip irrigation, tree rings, and watering stakes). Let's look at the benefits and drawbacks of each system, so you can make the best decision for your orchard.

Soaker Hoses

These consist of long porous hoses that allow water to seep out. Lying on top of the surface soil, water is distributed along the length of the tube. Advantages of using soaker hoses include not having to deal with clogs, their easy installation, and the small investment required for the set up. Moreover, the installation process is fairly easy and requires minimal maintenance.

Some downsides of using soaker hoses include the loss of water due to run off and encouraging the growth of weeds. The system isn't customizable, offering low precision, and underground installation is not possible, which can be a problem if you value aesthetics.

Advantages

- Cost effective
- Excellent for water conservation
- Prevents fungal diseases
- Efficient and requiring minimum effort
- Multiple plants can be watered through a single spigot

Disadvantages

- Overwatering due to lack of control over how much water is released
- Prone to getting damaged and require replacement every few seasons

Drip Irrigation

Drip irrigation consists of an extensive network of tubes with tiny holes, running throughout the garden. This allows the distribution of water to the plants in a slow and controlled manner. Unlike sprinklers, which cover large areas, drip irrigation carries small amounts of water to precise locations such as the root zone. Drip irrigation comes in various forms such as drip lines and tapes.

Drip Line

Drip lines are made of sturdy, round tubing that can last several years. They are extremely customizable and user friendly. You can buy drip lines with emitters to water plants at different locations in your garden.

Drip Tape

Drip tapes consist of flat tubing that works great directly under the soil's surface. It isn't as durable as drip lines, lasting only a few seasons at most, and requires a pressure reducer to function properly.

Now let's look at the pros and cons of drip irrigation.

Advantages

- Saves water by delivering controlled amounts to precise locations by the use of pressure regulators
- Encourages plant growth
- Suppresses weeds
- Prevents fungal diseases and infestations of pests
- Customizable

- Takes up less time since it can be put on a timer to water at regular intervals

Disadvantages

- Can require a significant up front investment and extensive planning
- Requires regular maintenance since the emitters can get clogged
- Some people may find the installation process frustrating

Micro sprinklers

Micro sprinklers operate at low pressure, dispersing droplets that mimic raindrops. These gadgets are much more efficient than traditional sprinklers, which tend to spray the tree bark, promoting disease and rot. In contrast, micro sprinklers come with deflectors that give the spray of water a downward trajectory. This is particularly helpful for young trees. However, as the tree matures, the deflector can be removed, allowing full spray.

Let's look at some pros and cons of using a micro sprinkler:

Advantages

- Covers a large area, reaching the root zone
- Uses large volumes of water, shortening watering cycles
- Prevents freeze damage
- Offers deflectors to keep the bark dry
- Easy to install

Disadvantages

- Uses a large amount of water
- Prone to insects developing nests in its spinners

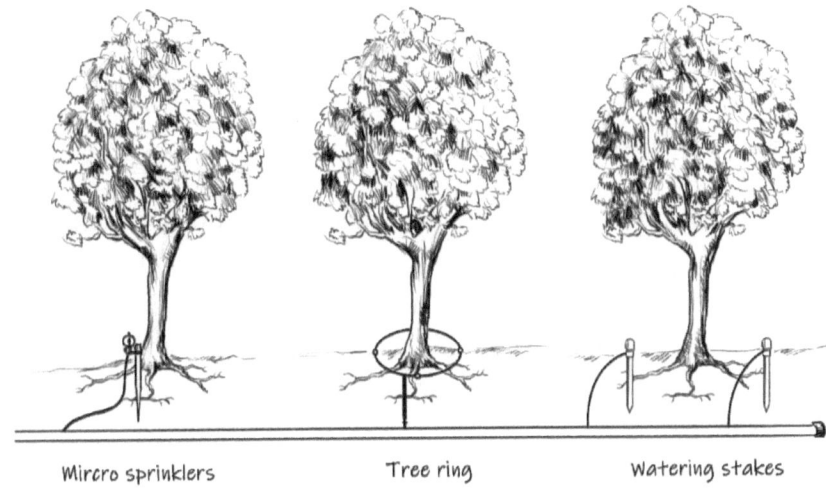

Figure 9: Different methods of orchard irrigation

Tree Rings

Tree rings consist of drip lines arranged in a ring pattern around the tree. They are generally considered a more water-efficient option than micro and traditional sprinklers. The water travels through the soil via emitters, reaching the plants directly. The water is absorbed deep into the soil through capillary action, covering the root zone and fulfilling the tree's moisture requirements.

Let's look at some pros and cons of using a tree ring:

Advantages

- Provides water to all sides of the root zone
- Delivers moisture directly to the soil without any loss due to evaporation or run-off
- Offers a variety of ring sizes for different trees
- Much more economical than the other options

Disadvantages
- Does not provide sufficient coverage in sandy soils
- Takes a longer time to install
- May get damaged by tools while working the landscape

Watering Stakes

A great method to achieve deep irrigation is installing watering stakes. They come in various sizes and are pushed into the soil near the tree's root zone. The stakes feature an internal filter to keep small rocks, pests, dirt, and debris out. While their use is not as widespread as the other two methods, they're particularly useful for irrigating bigger, older trees.

A drip emitter, uncapped microtubing, and garden hoses are all options to supply water to the stakes. To achieve this you'll have to place the hose, tubing, or emitter over the stake, lift the cap, turn on the water supply, and secure the cap.

Let's look at some pros and cons of using a watering stake.

Advantages
- Provides deep, thorough irrigation
- Aerates the soil
- Durable
- Works over a wide variety of tree sizes
- Loses very little water through evaporation or run-off

Disadvantages
- Can be costly
- Labor intensive
- Can't be easily moved from one location to another

Fruit Tree Nutrition

Balanced nutrition is crucial for the success of your orchard. Knowing the right nutrients and delivering them to the fruit trees at the right time can make all the difference. Let's look at the nutritional requirements of fruit trees, so you can have a bountiful harvest.

Choosing the Right Fertilizer

In total, plants need 16 nutrients to survive. However, you may have only heard of three main nutrients required for plant growth: nitrogen (N), phosphorous (P), and potassium (K). Nitrogen helps the leaves grow, phosphorus encourages root growth, while potassium is excellent for water retention and flower and fruit development. Different concentrations of N-P-K can be used to achieve the desired results. For example, foliage plants require greater concentration of nitrogen, while a higher percentage of potassium is required for flowering plants. Table 1 shows the effects of different nutrient deficiencies on fruit trees.

Table 1. Possible fruit tree problems due to excessive or deficient mineral concentrations (BC Fruit Tree Production Guide, n.d.).

Nutrient	Concent-ration	Problem
Nitrogen (N)	High	Storage rots, soft fruit, poor color, breakdown, bitter pit
	Low	Small fruit, increased risk of winter injury, biennial bearing, premature ripening
Phosphorus (P)	Low	Soft fruit and susceptibility to damage at low temperatures in some varieties

Potassium (K)	High	Bitter pit, breakdown
	Low	Lack of color and flavor, increased risk of winter injury and spring frosts
Calcium (Ca)	Low	Storage rots, fruit easily damaged, breakdown, bitter pit, early ripening, poor visual appearance
Magnesium (Mg)	High	Bitter pit, soft scald in some types
	Low	Shrunken fruit, premature ripening, preharvest drop
Boron (B)	High	Early ripening, preharvest drop, breakdown, damaged buds
	Low	Small, deformed fruit, presence of drought spot, fruit cracking, early ripening and preharvest drop

Unlike the azaleas or tomatoes growing in your garden, fruit trees don't require fertilizer every year and may require less fertilizer than the year before. To figure out how much feed your fruit trees really need, you must calculate their average growth rate. Find the growth ring on a branch, which is the area where the tree started growing the previous year. The tree's growth in the present year can be seen easily where the bark's color turns lighter.

Measure the distance between the new growth and the branch tip on at least six different branches. Add up the measurements and divide by six to calculate the average growth of the tree annually. Repeat the process for each tree. Now check Chart 5, which shows the average fruit tree growth. If your measurements fall in the middle or near the low end of your tree type, then you should go get the bag of fertilizer to replenish your soil's nutrient content. However, if the measurement leans toward the higher end, you can rest easy until next spring, because your trees have all the nutrients they need.

For example, six different branches on my peach tree show growth of 12, 16, 19, 17, 14, and 15 inches. Adding them up give me 93 inches. When I divide this number by 6, I get 15.5 inches. Looking at the chart, my measurement falls toward the lower end, which means it's time to give my peach tree a generous dose of fertilizer. Remember that overfeeding fruit trees may result in rapid growth that can weaken the tree, sapping its energy and keeping it from producing fruit.

Young Trees (non bearing)	Tart Cherry: 12" - 14" (30-35cm)
	Peach&Nectarine: 18" - 24" (45-60cm)
	Apple &Pear: 18" - 30" (45-75cm)
	Plum, Sweet Cherry &Apricot: 22" - 36"

MatureTrees (bearing)	Peach&Nectarine: 18" - 24" (45-60cm)
	Spur - Bearing Apple: 6" - 10" (15-25cm)
	Non-Spur Apple &Pear: 18" - 30" (45-75cm)
	Plum&Apricot: 8" (20cm)

Chart 5: Stage of tree based on average growth rate.

There are two main types of fertilizers: inorganic and organic. Inorganic fertilizers consist of mineral-based nutrients prepared in a refinery. These fertilizers are often reasonably priced and manufactured for immediate application. The percentage of the three macronutrients N-P-K are clearly mentioned on fertilizer bags. On the other hand, organic fertilizers contain organic matter in the form of manure or compost that has to be broken down by microorganisms to release nutrients, which are then taken up by the plant roots. So, the nutrients present in organic fertilizers are not readily available to plants as they are in soluble synthetic fertilizers.

There are various benefits of using organic fertilizer, including the gradual release of nutrients, which ensures a season-long supply. Remaining insoluble means minimal loss of nutrients to the environment and low risk of salt injury to plants. Moreover, the addition of organic matter improves soil health by increasing the soil's water-holding capacity and stimulating microbial activity.

Let's look at a few examples of organic fertilizers and their composition.

Blood Meal (NPK: 13.25-1-0.6)

This dry powder has the highest organic source of nitrogen and offers the added benefit of warding off deer, rabbits, and skunks.

Soybean Meal (NPK: 7-2-0)

This is a high-nitrogen fertilizer with trace amounts of phosphorus and calcium.

Cottonseed Meal (NPK: 6-0-4)

This is a great source of nitrogen, promoting growth of beneficial soil bacteria and slightly acidifying the soil.

Feather Meal (NPK: 13-0-0)

Widely considered the second-best organic source of nitrogen, it contains the protein keratin, which slowly releases nitrogen in the soil.

Alfalfa Meal (NPK: 3-2-3)

This is another slow-release nitrogen source.

Bone Meal (NPK: 3-15-0)

This adds essential phosphorus to the soil, promoting root, stem, flower, and fruit development.

Greensand (NPK: 0-0-3)

This is a naturally occurring mineral that supplements potassium in the soil and also behaves as a soil conditioner.

Compost and Kelp Meal

Fruit trees also require a wide range of macro/micronutrients and trace minerals for optimal growth. Compost and kelp meal are excellent options for delivering these to your fruit trees.

Step-by-Step Guide to Fertilizing Fruit Trees

Applying fertilizer may sound pretty straightforward; however, you can maximize the benefits by following a simple checklist. Here's a step-by-step guide to fertilizing your orchard:

1. Perform a soil test to determine nutrient concentration (refer to Chapter 1, Section 1.1).
2. Choose fertilizer based on the test results to supplement the lacking nutrients.
3. Apply fertilizer at the right time, usually early spring or late autumn.
4. Avoid direct contact with the tree trunk.
5. Water the tree afterward to allow the soil to absorb the nutrients.

Composting

Using compost can help increase the soil's organic matter content, ensuring orchard productivity. The addition of organic matter has multiple benefits such as improving root growth, soil structure, nutrient storage, soil pH, and water-holding capacity. Composts are different from manures and various other organic wastes, which can sometimes cause root burns. Moreover, direct application of manures and organic matter can increase fecal bacterial contaminants.

What makes compost distinct is that it is stabilized earthy matter. It is produced through the decomposition of massive quantities of fresh organic matter. Microbial activity is the first step to decompose the sugars, starches, and proteins, generating heat in the process, which kills fecal bacteria, pathogens, insects, and most weed seeds. Once most of the decomposed material has been utilized, microbial activity drops and the compost is considered stable.

Compost can be created from a range of feedstocks including manures, yard trimmings, kitchen wastes, spoiled hay, wood wastes, and prunings. You can make compost at home by following the steps below:

1. Layer moist green materials such as kitchen scraps or fresh garden prunings at the base of a large bin.
2. Add dry ingredients such as fallen leaves, crumpled newspaper, or shredded paper.
3. Shred the material as finely as possible to encourage quick degradation.
4. Aerate the mixture by adding more dry ingredients if it gets too wet or begins to smell.
5. Add some water if the mixture feels too dry in summer.

Mulching

Layers of decaying leaves and debris tend to naturally build up on the soil. Microbes break down this material, enriching the soil and boosting plant health. The process reintroduces nitrogen and other nutrients to the soil while slowing loss of water through evaporation. Mulching is the practice of covering the soil's surface with material such as leaf rankings and chipped up trees. Using organic mulches can also reduce the need for too-frequent watering; however, mulch thickness has to be at least two inches to slow down the evaporation of water.

When organic matter breaks down, it improves the overall soil health, making clay or compacted soil loose and adding micronutrients such as iron. It can help keep the roots warm during the frigid winter and cool during the scorching summer heat. Moreover, it draws earthworms to loamy soil and prevents weeds. Each fall, I apply a thick layer of mulch to my fruit trees, in addition to fifteen to forty percent chicken manure. At a depth of two inches, I spread generous amounts of mulch around the perimeter of the tree canopy, known as the dripline, taking care to stay away from the trunk to avoid root rot.

The Takeaway

We started off this chapter by learning complicated tree vocabulary and delved into secrets of finding healthy trees. We learned about the different kinds of rootstocks available at nurseries and discussed the when, where, and how of planting trees. By now, we know the important role of staking in protecting young trees and the various irrigation practices we can choose from to water our orchard. We've covered the nutritional requirements of fruit trees and the different fertilizers available. Finally, we discussed two extremely beneficial practices: mulching and composting.

Now that we know what it takes to make our orchard thrive, let's dive into another crucial aspect of growing trees: pruning. So get your shears ready; it's time to snip away the old and withered branches to make your trees shine.

CHAPTER 4

The Art of Shaping Trees

Training and pruning helps fruit trees grow into a proper shape and form. Well trained and pruned trees yield a plentiful harvest and have longer life spans. This is primarily due to stronger frameworks that support fruit production. Meanwhile, improperly trained trees tend to have upright branches, resulting in frequent limb breakage when laden with heavy fruits. This may reduce the tree's productivity and significantly shorten its life. Other advantages of pruning and training trees include open canopies allowing maximum sunlight penetration, increased air circulation, decreased risk of infection or disease, and well-shaped, aesthetically pleasing trees.

Since these two practices are closely related, let's analyze the difference between training and pruning.

Training Vs. Pruning

Traditionally, pruning has been the preferred method to maintain fruit tree form and structure. However, tree training is another efficient way to achieve the same result. While pruning involves removal of parts of a tree, the practice of training directs tree growth in a desired shape or form and is a prerequisite for proper tree development. Furthermore, pruning is performed mostly during the winter during a period of dormancy. On the contrary, training mostly takes place during the summer during a period of active growth.

Training encourages the development of strong tree structure capable of supporting heavy fruits. It also helps trees bear fruit at an early age. Meanwhile, pruning reduces the size of the tree, making it more manageable to care for and harvest. It also strengthens trees, promotes branching, and increases fruit production.

If you're new to growing trees, the different terminologies used for pruning may sound confusing. Figure 10 illustrates a tree and its various parts in relation to pruning. I've included a glossary of the tree parts that you're bound to encounter when you take up the shears. Remember that some common words such as twig, shoot, limb, and branch are used interchangeably. However, a twig or a shoot is mostly used for young growth while limb and branch is used for older, more mature growth.

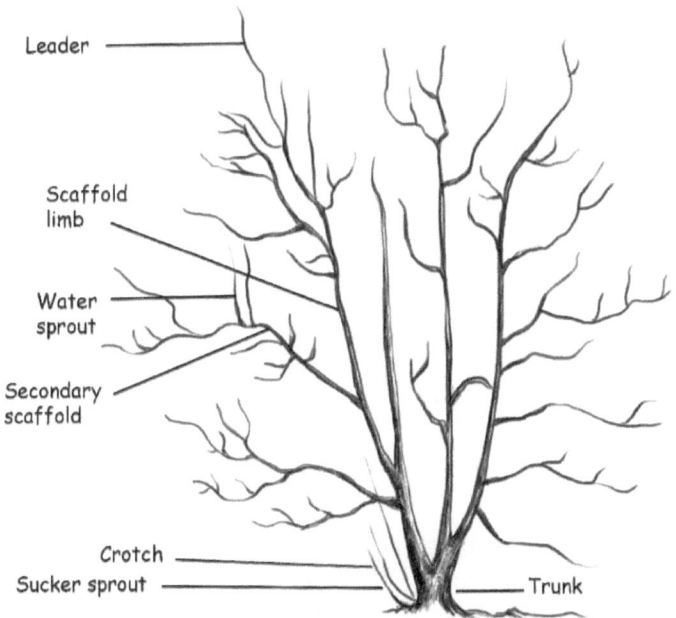

Common terms used in pruning and training fruit trees

Figure 10: Different parts of a tree

General Guidelines for Training

- Begin training during planting time.
- Prune unwanted shoots in the summer when they're young and small in size.
- Train mostly by limb positioning instead of pruning (We will discuss this technique in more detail in Chapter 4).
- Adhere to a training program consistently.

General Guidelines For Pruning

- Start by pruning all the fruit and nut trees so the tops are proportionate with the roots.
- Save heavy pruning for mature trees, especially if they show slow growth.
- Prune the top more heavily than the lower branches.
- Prune after the early winter freeze has passed or during autumn.
- Thin out the shoots growing at the branch's end in mature trees to boost the size and quality of fruit.

Protect the Branch Collar!

While pruning, it's important to save the branch collar without using wound dressings. Make sure to prune so you leave a stub as illustrated in Figure 11.

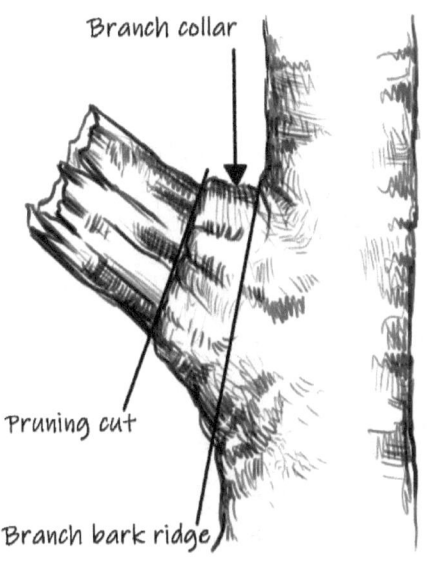

Figure 11: Branch collar

You must make sure the wound is no larger than strictly necessary. This can be achieved by cutting just outside the branch collar (the raised tissue found at the point connecting the base of each branch to the tree). The specialized cells in this area protect pruning wounds from wood rot fungi. Also, there's no clear evidence that wound dressings minimize risks of trees developing wood rot. However, early tree training can help you avoid large pruning wounds situated low in the tree, which can become infected.

Pruning Glossary

Branch Collar: Raised tissue at the bottom of each branch, containing specialized cells that protect pruning wounds from fungal infections.

Crotch Angle: The angle between the tree trunk and a limb. The sharpest crotch angles range from 45 to 60 degrees.

Crown: The base of the tree where the trunk meets the ground.

Head Cut/ Heading: A pruning cut that takes out a specific part of a branch.

Lateral Branch: The sideshoot of a branch, lying at a horizontal angle.

Leader: The topmost portion of a scaffold limb.

Scaffold Limb: The largest branch serving as the foundation of a tree.

Shoot: The length a branch achieves during one growing season.

Stub: A small portion of a branch remaining after pruning, which should always be avoided.

Sucker Sprout: A year old shoot growing from the root ball.

Terminal: The portion where a shoot ends.

Thinning Cut: A pruning cut that slices a branch from its point of origin.

Vertical Branch: A branch growing upright.

Water Sprout: A year-old shoot growing within a tree.

Types of Pruning Cuts

Depending on the weather, fruit trees can be pruned when dormant or a month or two before spring. Usually, pruning during the rainy season is a terrible idea, as it increases chances of fungal infection. A wide crotch angle and a height of at least two or more feet from the ground is necessary for using a branch as a permanent scaffold limb.

The first step involves removing dead, damaged, or diseased parts. Spot a cracked branch? Cut it. See some rust or scab? Snip it away. You want the trees to channel their energy toward the healthiest branches to have the best harvest. Any branches crossing or limping down should be pruned as well. Remove any sprouts originating from the tree trunk as well. It's also important to ensure you cut at an angle at the right location, which is the place where the branch meets the trunk.

Different types of prunings are used to achieve various results. Let's look at some of these types.

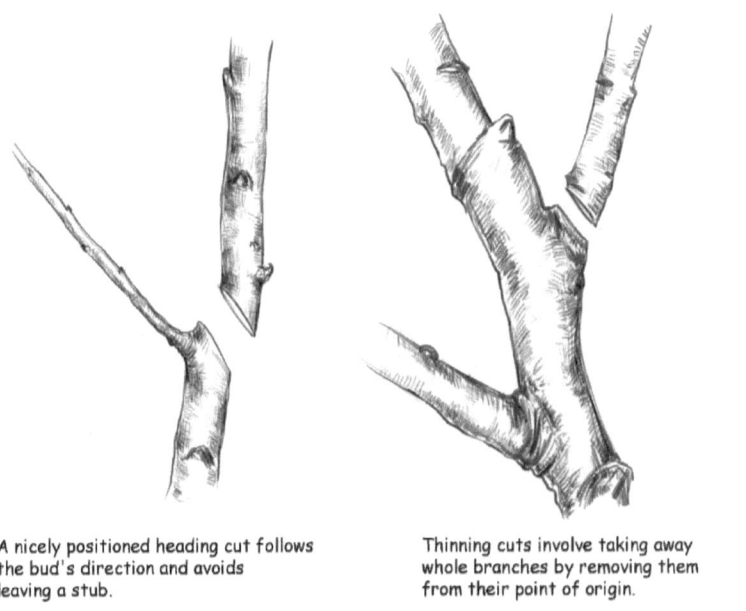

A nicely positioned heading cut follows the bud's direction and avoids leaving a stub.

Thinning cuts involve taking away whole branches by removing them from their point of origin.

Figure 12: Heading and thinning cuts.

Thinning Cut

A thinning cut takes out a whole branch, reducing it to a side shoot. This type of pruning doesn't invigorate trees compared to other cuts. For example, in Figure 13 the branches that require thinning have a gray outline.

On this well-developed branch, remove additional shoots towards the end

Figure 13: The branches with the gray outline require a thinning cut.

Heading Cut

This pruning style only removes the terminal area of a branch, promoting lower bud growth. When lateral branches are nearing one-year-old wood, the place near the cut is invigorated. The headed branch becomes much stronger, leading to lateral secondary branches 12 to 15 inches away. Older trees can be shaped by "mold and hold" cuts, which are de-invigorating heading cuts made when the wood is at least two years old. Young trees and branches subjected to heading cuts are referred to as "headed." Figure 14 illustrates the heading cuts.

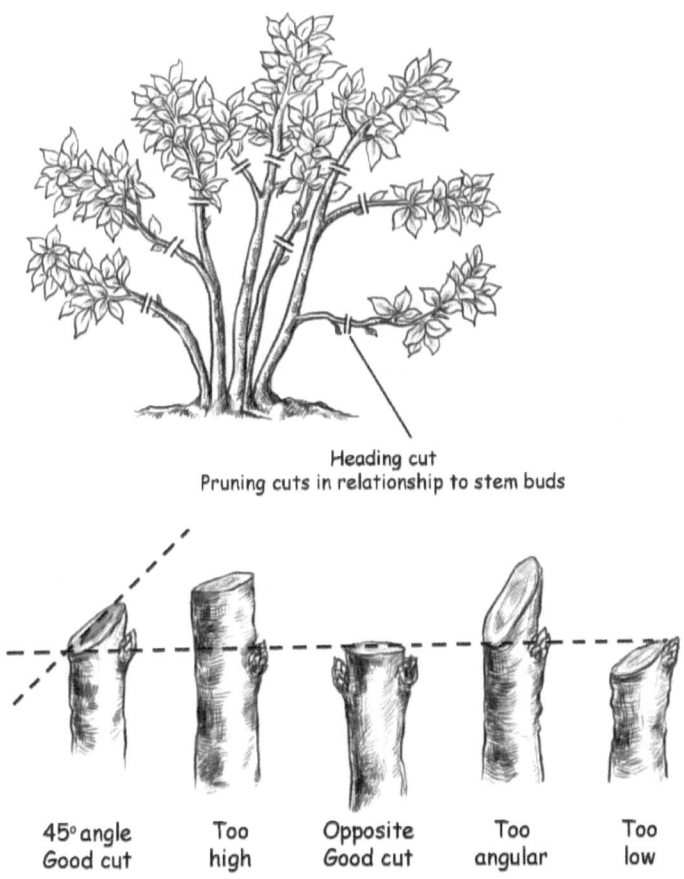

Figure 14: Different types of pruning cuts and angles.

Bench Cut

A bench cut targets vigorous, upright branches, reducing them to side branches similar in diameter to the branch pruned but less upright and growing outward. They are used to open the tree's center and spread the branches. When pruning, it's important to make clean, sharp cuts that heal quickly to minimize the risk of disease or insect infection.

The cuts should be made near the adjacent branch without leaving stubs. Also, horizontal cuts should be slightly angled so water does not accumulate on the wound.

Open Central Vs. Central Leader

You can't go wrong with open-center pruning. The vase-shaped structures created through this pruning method may seem familiar to most rose pruners. The form is often compared to an open palm with the fingers spread out.

Rapidly growing stone fruits such as peaches, plums, and nectarines respond well to open-center pruning. Their brittle branches are not suited to a central leader. Although in some cases, pruning the lower branches may fortify the trunk, creating a central leader. In such scenarios, the top buds grow vertically, transforming into the new center trunk from which side branches called laterals shoot out. The central leader method is usually used to strengthen fruit trees like cherries and apples, encouraging them to grow large. The shape of such trees tends to resemble a Christmas tree or a ballerina's skirt.

The pruning method you settle on ultimately depends on each individual tree. If vertical branches stubbornly remain vertical no matter what you try, your tree might be in need of a central leader. When trees are meant to be kept small, the choice between open center or central leader boils down to a matter of style rather than substance. We'll discuss both these methods in more detail in section 4.2 below. It takes four winters for trees to assume a central leader formation.

Figure 15 shows different growth stages of a tree. **A** represents a tree during its first winter after planting. At this stage, prune the most vigorous shoots on top if they exceed the length of two feet to encourage branching. **B**, **C**, and **D** depict the following three winters. Repeat the pruning process each year to prevent side branches from becoming dominant and encourage central leader formation.

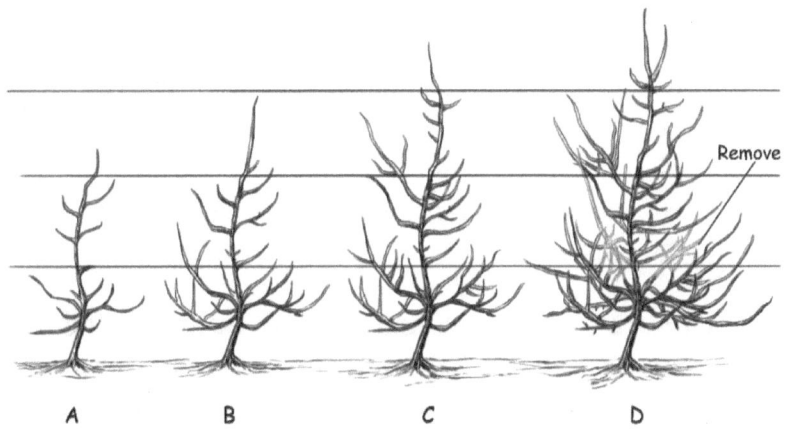

Figure 15: Different stages of tree development.

Step-By-Step Guide to Pruning

The first spring after hard pruning your trees is crucial, as this is when the tree breaks out of dormancy, budding below the pruning cuts. It doesn't take long for the top three or four buds to develop into scaffold branches by summer. Here are the steps you need to follow during the first spring and summer season:

1. **Cut down multiple leaf buds to one bud on each branch.** Use your fingers to snap multiple buds sprouting from a single leaf node, leaving behind only one. Do this around March or April then revisit the tree for more pruning in June.

2. **Remove the suckers from rootstocks.** Cut the limbs sprouting at or below the graft. Shoots coming out from the rootstock sap the plant's energy by redirecting resources away from the scion. Moreover, the branches emerging from the rootstocks don't produce decent fruit.

3. **Reconsider the current scaffold.** By early summer, young branches will begin assuming strength. Ideally, the top buds grow into well-formed scaffolds and the young tree develops three or four evenly spaced branches around the trunk. However, if the branches break or the top buds become

inactive, you'll have to make a clean 45-degree prune near the top branching bud. The cut will become the crotch of the tree. You can take this moment to wonder if the cut you made was low enough and consider dropping the scaffold for shorter tree height and more lower branching. If the idea of a lower scaffold appeals to you, make another clean cut at a 45-degree angle.

4. **Think about the arrangement of future scaffold limbs.** Remove one or two branches growing too close to one another. Leave the shoots emerging above the graft even if they're low as they belong to the scion and will bear fruit. While pruning, keep angled branches and do away with limbs that are too horizontal or vertical. This is because at about 45 degrees, a branch is horizontal enough to bear fruit and angled enough to support its weight.

5. **Shorten the limbs.** Remove the extraneous branches, reducing the remaining branches at least half to a bud facing the direction you want the limb to grow.

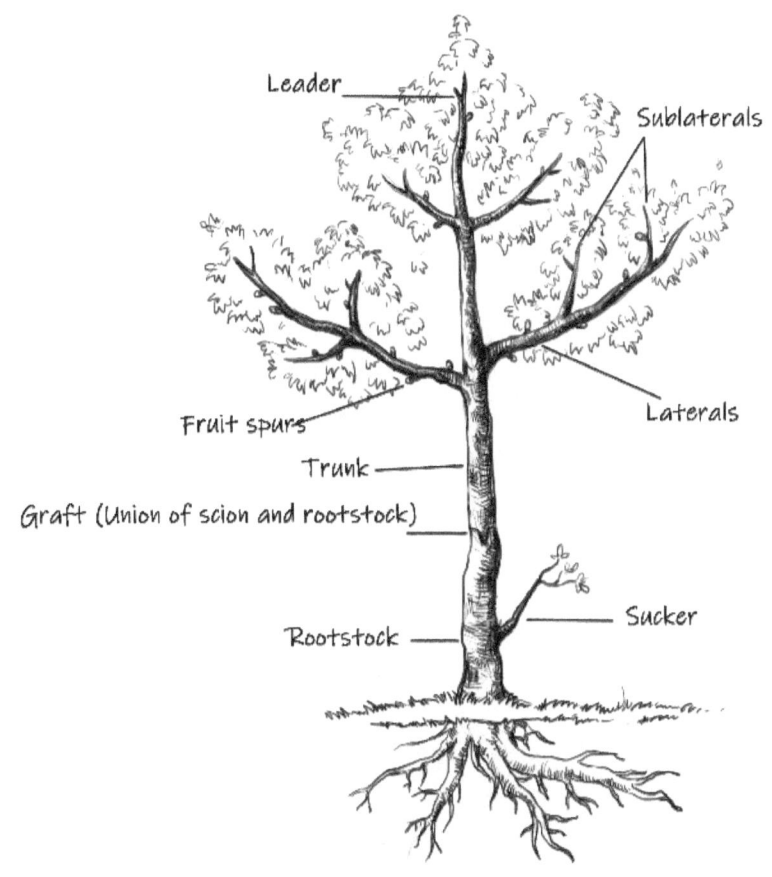

Figure 16: Common pruning terms.

Training Your Trees

So what shape should you choose for training your fruit trees? While there is no definite answer to that question, there are multiple training shapes to choose from. In this book, we will focus on the central leader and open center training systems. Regardless of the training and pruning system you choose, remember that the goal is to help maximize your trees' longevity, productivity, and fruit quality.

Open Center Training

The first winter after planting your tree, select three or four branches from the main scaffold branch. Prune the other branches so there are no competing limbs, or head them by cutting one fourth to one third of their length. After removing large branches, cut the branch on the underside in the middle, then perform the top cut. Make sure not to leave any stubs. Keep the trees small by pruning moderately each year.

It takes a total of four winters for a tree to achieve open center formation. Figure 17 represents a tree through different growth stages. **A** shows a tree during its first winter. As mentioned above, select three or four shoots and prune the rest. The branches you've selected will form the scaffold branch and should be at least eight inches apart. **B** depicts the second winter. Choose one or two more branches at this point and prune the rest. Scaffold selection usually ends by the third winter, as shown in **C**. Lastly, **D** shows an open center formation with four main scaffold branches distributed evenly around the trunk.

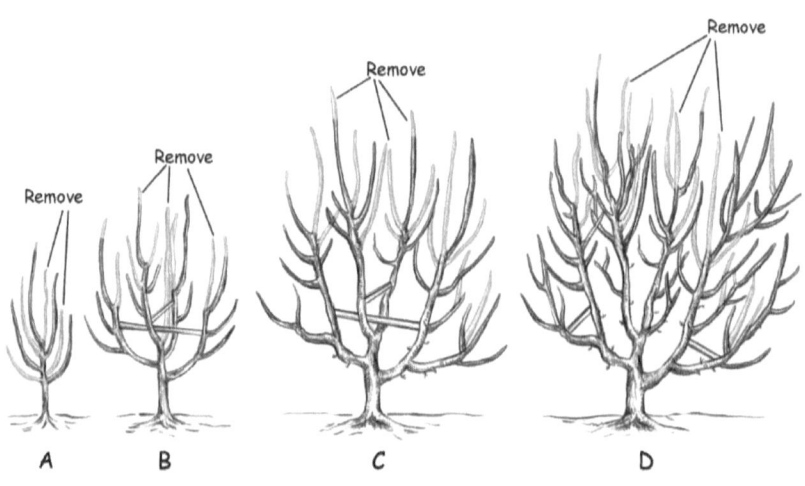

Figure 17: Pruning trees at different growth stages.

Central Leader Training

You can head trees with sparse branches at 24 to 30 inches above the ground. Central leader training requires choosing a strong branch near the center. In spring or early summer, cut shoots near the leader, which might compete with the leader. During winter, when the tree is dormant, cut one-third of the leader branch and remove competing branches. Each year, prune the tree to get rid of upright branches and encourage limbs that are spread out.

Repeat the above process in the next two seasons, so there are no side branches that could compete with the central leader. Dwarf apple varieties with naturally wide-angled branches such as Liberty won't require heading or spreading; however, those with narrow crotches or vertical limbs such as Delicious and Newton's Will.

Espalier Training

Espalier training encourages the trees to develop in two dimensions only. You can use it for your home orchard to save space and make it more aesthetically pleasing. The technique creates trees that are easier to pick, prune, and spray for pests. By using this method, you can easily grow dwarf apple trees on posts or wire trellis in hedgerows. The posts may range from six to ten feet above the ground. While treated posts are usually the best, strong untreated four by four cedar posts can work too.

Start by anchoring the posts' end against another post. Drive the posts several feet in the soil at opposing angles. Take a galvanized 12 gauge wire and tie the main trunk. The lowest part of the wire should be at least four feet above the ground. Use big loops allowing the trunk to grow. Tree trunks fastened to trellis wires with $5/8$-inch box staples will graft to the wire and not the girdle.

If each tree has its own individual posts, make sure they reach the height of six feet above the ground and push them two feet in the ground. The diameter of the wooden stakes should be two inches or more. While training the tree, choose buds that will grow into branches at the correct height and prune the tree above them. As the new shoots appear, fix them to the training wires. Figure 18 shows what espalier training looks like.

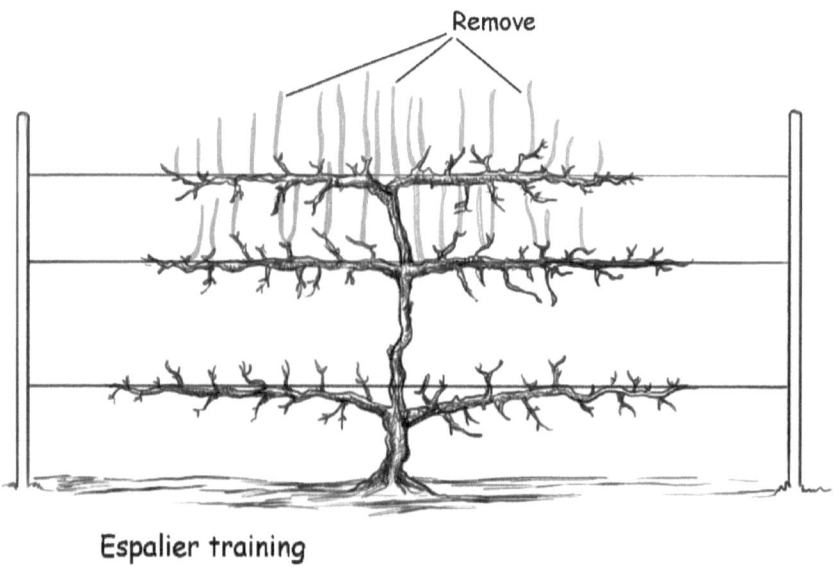

Espalier training

Figure 18: Espalier training fruit trees.

Palmette

Palmette is a pattern of espalier training. It allows the development of the lowest branches first at an angle of 30 degrees. Gradually, the angle is widened to 45-50 degrees once the branches achieve the desired length. At this point, gardeners should head the central leader. Develop branches located high up in the tree by keeping them short and more spread out than the one below. A distance of 18 inches between the branches is ideal. Figure 19 illustrates the palmette pattern of espalier training.

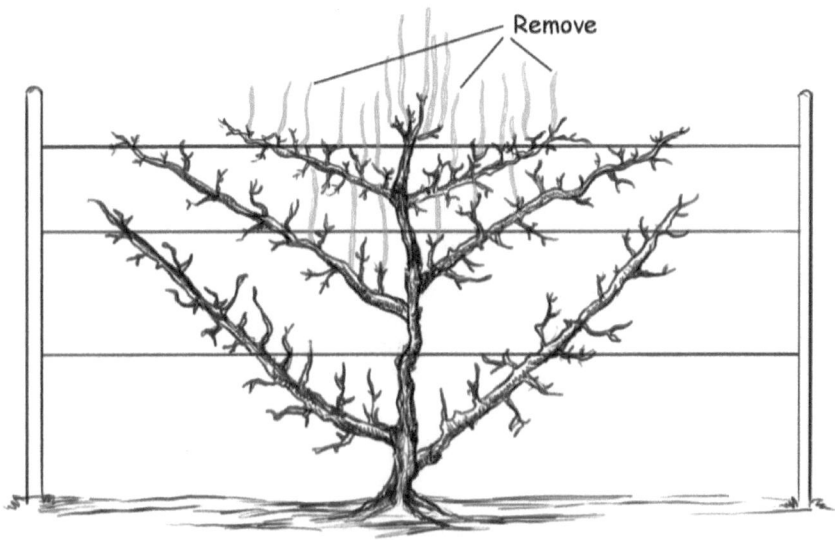

Figure 19: Palmette training fruit trees.

Bringing Old Trees to Life

Getting rid of old and diseased parts encourages new growth. If the trunk is sound, without any holes or rotted center, you have a chance to save it. Pruning can be a great way to rejuvenate dying trees. If you happen to find old, abandoned trees on your property, here are some questions to ask yourself before kick-starting the restoration process:

- Does it appear healthy with minimal damage?
- Does it produce your desired fruit?
- Does its location fit into your garden plan?
- Can you keep it small and in good shape?
- Will you be able to care for it properly, if it remains large?

Old, forgotten trees tend to become home for insects and diseases, which can spread to other trees. If you've resolved to restore your old fruit tree, here are the steps you should take:

1. Perform a heavy, corrective prune when the tree is dormant.
2. Reshape the tree during the first year. Shorten it by six to eight feet, if it's over 20 feet tall.
3. Cut the main scaffold limbs.
4. Prune the upper third of the tree, getting rid of dead, crossing, and hanging branches.
5. Remove vigorous top shoots during the summer of the following year.
6. Leave a few minor branches at the lower part of the trunk that don't provide too much shade. This will encourage the tree to produce new fruit wood.
7. Cut down half of the new branches on the top in the third year. Look for shoots growing near the previous heavy pruning cuts.
8. Remove the strongest shoots first.
9. Shape the tree during the third dormant period and shorten it by one or two feet.
10. Spread the newly formed wood, making sure all the branches are easily accessible for pruning, spraying, and harvesting.

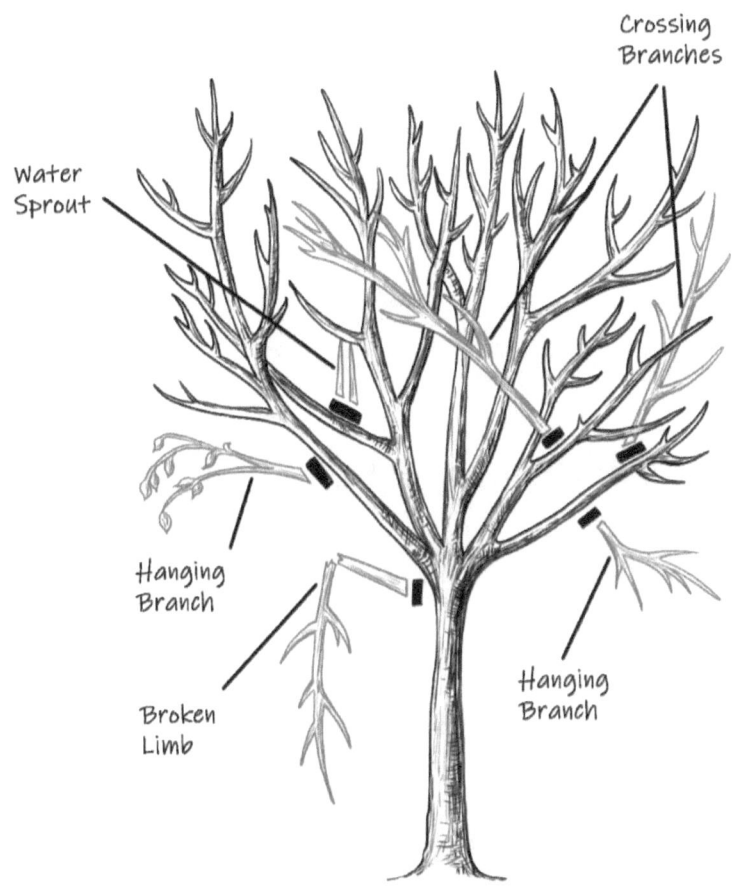

Figure 20: Rejuvenating old trees through pruning.

The Takeaway

Pruning is a great way to keep trees healthy and enhance fruit production. When combined with training, it ensures maximum sunlight distribution, improved airflow, and increased tree strength. We discussed the various methods of training trees and different kinds of pruning methods. Finally, we learned how pruning techniques can be used to restore old trees. Now that we've covered the basics of shaping trees, let's move on to pests and disease that could pose a threat to your orchard.

CHAPTER 5

Organic Pest and Disease Management

Healthy plants are strong enough to ward off potential problems. By fulfilling your plants' essential requirements, choosing varieties suited to your climate, and nipping problems in the bud, you can create an orchard that self-corrects.

Steps to Maintain a Healthy Orchard

Keeping your garden healthy requires a decent level of care and observation. Here are some steps to keep your garden functioning at an optimum level.

1. **Keep a Lookout for Bugs:** Regularly inspect your plants for signs of pest or insect infestations. Wilting, holes or bites in leaves, discolored spots, leaf dropping, yellowing leaves, or drooping branches are some indications that your tree might be battling a foreign invader.

2. **Prune Damaged or Diseased Part:** Timely pruning of wounded or disease branches can limit the spread of disease and prevent problems from multiplying. Injured limbs can become infected during winter. Since the tree is dormant, the disease or pest can easily become established, creating severe problems during spring.

3. **Water Properly:** Most pathogens thrive in warm, moist, and dark environments. Choosing watering methods that limit moisture retention on the foliage, such as soaker hoses and drip irrigation, can help prevent this. Meanwhile, well-draining soil can further protect the roots from root-rotting fungi.

4. **Maintain Your Soil's Nutrient Content:** Well-fed trees with access to all the nutrients required for their growth are in a better position of fighting off disease. The addition of manure, compost, and planting more cover crops can help improve the soil's nutrient content. Tilling the soil annually or biannually can also help break up compaction, making it easier for plants to absorb water and nutrients.

5. **Use Completely Composted Yard Waste:** The materials used in a compost pile don't decompose at the same rate. Although the high temperatures generated during composting kill bacteria and other pathogens, improper or incomplete composting can introduce infected plant debris to the soil.

Tackling Problems Head On

Some problems arise due to the changing weather. Some plants are more susceptible to certain pests and diseases. An attentive gardener catches problems in their early stages, taking corrective measures to prevent future damage. It's important to remember that insects and diseases are opportunists, attacking compromised plants. Plants undergoing stress from being placed at the wrong site or not receiving adequate care are at a greater risk of developing problems.

Sun-stressed or drought-stressed, elderly fruit trees can become infected by borers. The tiny insects tunnel deep in the bark, sapping the trees of energy and eventually killing them. Meanwhile, aphids feast on succulent new growth. Plums, cherries, and apricots are prone to developing gummosis, a condition commonly known as 'weeping sap,' due to water-logged soil. Trees receiving more shade than required become affected by mildew. Fire blight is a common bacterial disease affecting apple varieties. It gains entry through blossoms and causes the tree to wither. Temperature fluctuations increase the chances of developing this condition.

While some pests can certainly cause significant damage, your home garden doesn't need to be entirely pest free. It may sound counterintuitive but a moderate level of insects and pests in the garden contributes to its overall health. For instance, a mild infestation of whiteflies on citrus trees attracts Encarsia wasp, which keeps it from spreading. In my opinion, relying on natural systems is the best way to prevent disease in the long run and maintain garden health.

Generally, minor outbreaks of disease cause little harm, resolving on their own as the weather becomes more agreeable. Moreover, diseased or infected parts can be easily pruned, encouraging new growth. The use of chemical pesticides indiscriminately kills beneficial insects, leading to more problems down the road. If you think a particular tree in your garden is not doing well, here are some steps you can take to restore it back to health:

1. Evaluate the damage and prune the affected branches.
2. Create a checklist to keep track of the damage and gauge whether the problem is becoming stable or worse.
3. Ask yourself if environmental conditions (drought, weather, or too much shade) are to blame.
4. Look up the tree's essential requirements (water, sunlight, nutrition) and ask yourself if it's lacking in any area. Readjust your gardening method and see if the situation improves.
5. Look for signs of pests if tree health continues to deteriorate.

In the case of pest infestation, there are various methods, either physical, biological or chemical, that you can use to bring the situation under control. Let's look at some of these.

Physical Controls

Mechanical methods of control eliminate pests usually without disrupting beneficial ecosystems. These include tilling for suppressing weed growth, removing weeds by pulling, pruning infected plant parts, installing barriers and traps, adding mulches, and manually removing insects or cankers.

Biological Controls

This involves using natural enemies to deter pest populations. Using biological controls is the foundation of Integrated Pest Management (IPM). Every insect or pest has a natural predator. Making them a part of your garden ecosystem allows you to regulate pest populations. For example, in 2007, light brown apple moths caused significant damage to apple crops in California. In addition to other methods, researchers tried increasing ladybug and lacewing populations in the area. Let's look at some examples of biological controls.

- **Predatory Arthropods**

  These are the beneficial insects in your garden. Spiders, beetles, lacewings, and some predatory mites prey on a wide range of pests such as thrips, white flies, aphids, and other soft bodied organisms.

- **Parasitic Nematodes**

  Parasitoids are insects that lay eggs inside a host. Their larvae feed on the host, eventually killing it. They target specific insect populations, sparing others. For example, colorless roundworms can be used to regulate populations of caterpillars, grubs, cutworms, thrips, crown borers, gnats, beetles, and fungus gnats.

Chemical Controls

Pesticides are chemicals that make the habitat lethally toxic, killing large swathes of potentially harmful insects and pests. They are classified on the basis of the pests they target, such as insecticides, fungicides, and bactericides. They can be further divided into synthetic (designed in labs) or organic (naturally occuring).

Inorganic and Organic Pesticides

When it comes to choosing chemical controls, it's best to try out the least toxic option first. This can be something as simple as handpicking the pests or insects, if possible. Here are some options to choose from to keep your orchard thriving:

Inorganic Pesticides

- **Diatomaceous Earth (DE)**

DE is another excellent option containing silica. It is commercially available in powder form, which can be dusted or sprayed on plants. It draws fats and oils from the insect's exoskeleton, drying it up and effectively killing it. An advantage of using DE is that it remains active for a long time, protecting the plants from future attacks.

- **Potassium Bicarbonate**

This is usually combined with horticultural oil and other additives to increase its spread. You can easily prepare it on your own or buy it from the market. Spray when you detect the first signs of disease to limit its spread or as a precautionary measure to prevent problems. The bicarbonates in the solution create a highly alkaline environment, suppressing fungal growth. There is the possibility of leaf burn after application, especially in harsh sunlight.

- **Neonicotinoids**

Neonicotinoids are a class of synthetic insecticides designed as a more targeted and less toxic alternative to traditional pesticides. Acting on insect nervous systems by binding to nicotinic acetylcholine receptors, neonicotinoids lead to paralysis and death. They're effective against a broad spectrum of pests.

However, their use has raised significant environmental concerns, particularly regarding their impact on pollinators like bees. Some regions have imposed restrictions or bans, prompting a reevaluation of neonicotinoid usage in favor of more sustainable Integrated Pest Management strategies that consider the potential risks to non-target organisms while addressing pest control needs.

- **Organophosphates**

Organophosphates are a class of synthetic pesticides widely used for insect control in agriculture and pest management. They include malathion, diazinon, and chlorpyrifos, which inhibit cholinesterase activity, an essential enzyme in the nervous system of insects. By disrupting neurotransmission, organophosphates lead to the accumulation of acetylcholine, resulting in the overstimulation of nerve cells and eventual paralysis in targeted pests.

Despite their effectiveness in controlling a broad spectrum of insects, organophosphates are associated with environmental and health concerns. Their non-selective nature can harm beneficial insects, wildlife, and aquatic organisms, and they pose risks to human health through exposure. Due to these concerns, regulatory measures and restrictions on organophosphate use have been implemented in various regions, promoting the adoption of alternative, less harmful pest management strategies.

Organic Pesticides

- **Bacillus Thuringiensis (Bt)**

More than 80 Bt species function as pesticides that are sprinkled or dusted on the plants. It works as a stomach poison when ingested by insects, causing them to starve and die. The bacteria target specific hosts, leaving other animals unharmed. Hornworms, caterpillar pests, and corn earworms are some pests susceptible to Bt.

While it is extremely effective against a wide range of hosts, some may find its slow-acting process a disadvantage. Moreover, the bacteria breaks down more rapidly in harsh sunlight and can sometimes harm butterfly larvae. Carefully reading label instructions and avoiding overuse can mitigate the aforementioned risks.

- **Neem Oil**

Composed of only two ingredients, azadirachtin and salannin, the mixture can be sprayed on the trees to prevent pest infestations. It disrupts the insect's hormones, stunting its growth and thereby killing it. While it's non-toxic in nature, it washes away in rain, may cause burns in harsh sunlight, and is slow acting.

- **Horticultural Oil**

Containing highly refined petroleum oil, this is mixed with water and sprayed on the trees. The oil forms a layer on the surface of the leaves, suffocating and killing insects. It's non-toxic and doesn't leave any residue. While it is extremely effective against soft-bodied insects, it can sometimes cause leaf burns.

- **Pyrethrins**

Available in powder form, this insecticide can be sprinkled on the leaves to poison predatory insects. It's fast acting with low toxicity. However, being a broad-spectrum insecticide, it can kill a wide range of insects, including honey bees.

- **Sabadilla**

This contains ground seeds of sabadilla lily, commercially available as a fine powder that is used as a spray. An effective stomach poison against bugs of the Hemiptera order, it can also harm bees and other animals.

- **Rotenone**

Formed using the roots of tropical legumes, this is usually sprinkled on plants. Its low residual effect and quick breakdown in sunlight are counted as pros. However, it is a broad spectrum pesticide, mildly toxic to humans upon ingestion. It's best to apply it in the evening, when beneficial insects like bees are less active.

- **Bordeaux Mixture**

This contains copper sulfate and lime mixed with water. An effective bactericide and fungicide, it has been used to control garden diseases for decades. The solution sticks to the plants in rainy weather, making it an excellent fungicide. Some diseases that it is effective against include fire blight on apples and pears, downy and powdery mildew on grapes, peacock spot on olives and walnut blight on walnuts.

- **Insecticidal Soaps**

These contain sodium or potassium salts mixed with fatty acids. The soap should come in direct contact with the pest, allowing the fatty acids to penetrate its outer covering and causing its death. It leaves no residue and is widely considered a safe, non-toxic option. However, it can cause burns to the plant if used during high temperatures or exposure to harsh sunlight. Moreover, it isn't effective against adult beetle pests with hard shells. Always read the label before using insecticidal soap to check whether a particular plant is sensitive to any ingredient.

Know the Enemy: Common Pests and Diseases

Let's round up the usual suspects and familiarize ourselves with common enemies in the garden.

Aphids

- Affect most fruit trees during early summer
- Transmit viruses
- You should handpick them whenever you spot them

- Encourage ladybug population in your garden

Bacterial Canker

- Affects trees of the Prunus family (almonds, cherries, plums, peaches, apples, apricots, and nectarines)
- Emerges as small brown spots that eventually turn into large holes
- Deforms leaves causing discoloration and withering
- Kills branches and can easily kill the tree
- You should prune affected areas and burn them
- Use copper-based fungicides like the Bordeaux mixture during late summer
- Repeat as autumn begins

Blossom Wilt

- Affects stone fruits, pears, and apples
- Causes withered, rotting blossoms
- Invades the trees through the leaves
- Weakens the trees, making them susceptible to attacks
- You should prune and incinerate affected areas
- Apply Bordeaux mixture

Botrytis

- Affects any part of the trees, appearing as a gray, felty mold
- Occurs due to poor ventilation and damp conditions
- Can affect grapes before they ripen
- You should prune the affected areas with your hands and apply an appropriate fungicide

Brown Rot

- Creates brown spots, affecting a wide range of trees such as pears, apples, and stone fruits
- Enters the trees through sites of injury
- You should prune and destroy affected fruits or tree parts

Brown Scale
- Leads to yellowing and dying leaves
- Caused by a tiny sap-sucking insect
- You should treat with organic pesticides

Codling Moth
- Damages fruits after its larvae tunnels to the fruit's core
- Makes the tree vulnerable to other diseases
- You can use pheromone traps to catch adult moths in late spring

Coral Spot
- Affects fruits such as figs and currants
- Thrives in damp conditions through pruning injuries
- Appears as orange pink spots on dead wood
- You should prune and destroy the affected parts immediately after detecting this issue

Downy Mildew
- Appears as gray downy growth on the underside and yellow spots on the upper side of leaves
- Caused by poor ventilation
- You should prune and burn infected leaves
- Apply a sulfur based spray

Fire Blight

- Blackens leaves, shoots, and flowers of pears, apples, and quince, giving them a burnt look
- You should prune and extra 20 inches above the affected area to ensure healthy growth
- Disinfect secateurs immediately after pruning and burn the cuttings

Leaf Curl

- Affects peaches, almonds, and nectarines, distorting the leaves
- Causes leaf dropping, and reduced fruiting
- You can apply Bordeaux mixture as a remedy

Mealy Bugs

- Caused by small white insects that may appear on the leaf axils and midribs of figs, grapes, and citrus fruits
- Produces a sticky residue on the leaves, which can turn into dark mold
- You can treat it with organic sprays

Nectria Canker

- Affects apples, causing the bark to crack and peel
- Prune affected areas and disinfect secateurs
- Burn diseased parts and apply Bordeaux mixture to treat

Rust Plums

- Affects pears and berries
- Causes bright orange blisters on the underside of leaves that gradually turn brown
- You should prune and incinerate the affected leaves

Scab

- Appears as brown or pale green spots on leaves and shoots, leading to deformed fruits

- You can apply organic pesticides such as insecticidal soaps

Wasps

- Bore holes in apples, pears, plums, strawberries and raspberries
- You can install wasp traps around the trees and cover the fruits as they ripen

Winter Moths

- Damage leaves, flowers, and buds of cherries, plums, and pears
- Apply sticky strips around the tree trunk
- Can get eaten by birds and controlled naturally
- If the problem persists, you could spray insecticidal soaps

Plants with strong odors serve as a natural deterrent for pests. A blend of herbs and alliums can discourage pests, and some may even draw predatory insects. Herbs and alliums that thrive in shaded areas offer an extra advantage by growing near the tree trunk, enhancing protection. They are also wonderfully useful in the kitchen!

Plants that deter pests include: basil, garlic, savory, dill, catnip, thyme, onions, leeks, borage ,lavender, chives, lemon balm, fennel, oregano, lemongrass, hyssop, cilantro, bergamot, lovage, sage, ginger, turmeric, marjoram, anise, lemon verbena, spearmint, peppermint, rosemary, chervil, tarragon, parsley.

When Should You Spray?

Even with all the above information at your disposal, you might wonder when is the right time to bring out the big guns. Whether you choose natural or synthetic options, spraying pesticides should preferably be treated as a last resort. The charts below will help you figure out the appropriate time and treatment to use for your trees at different growth stages.

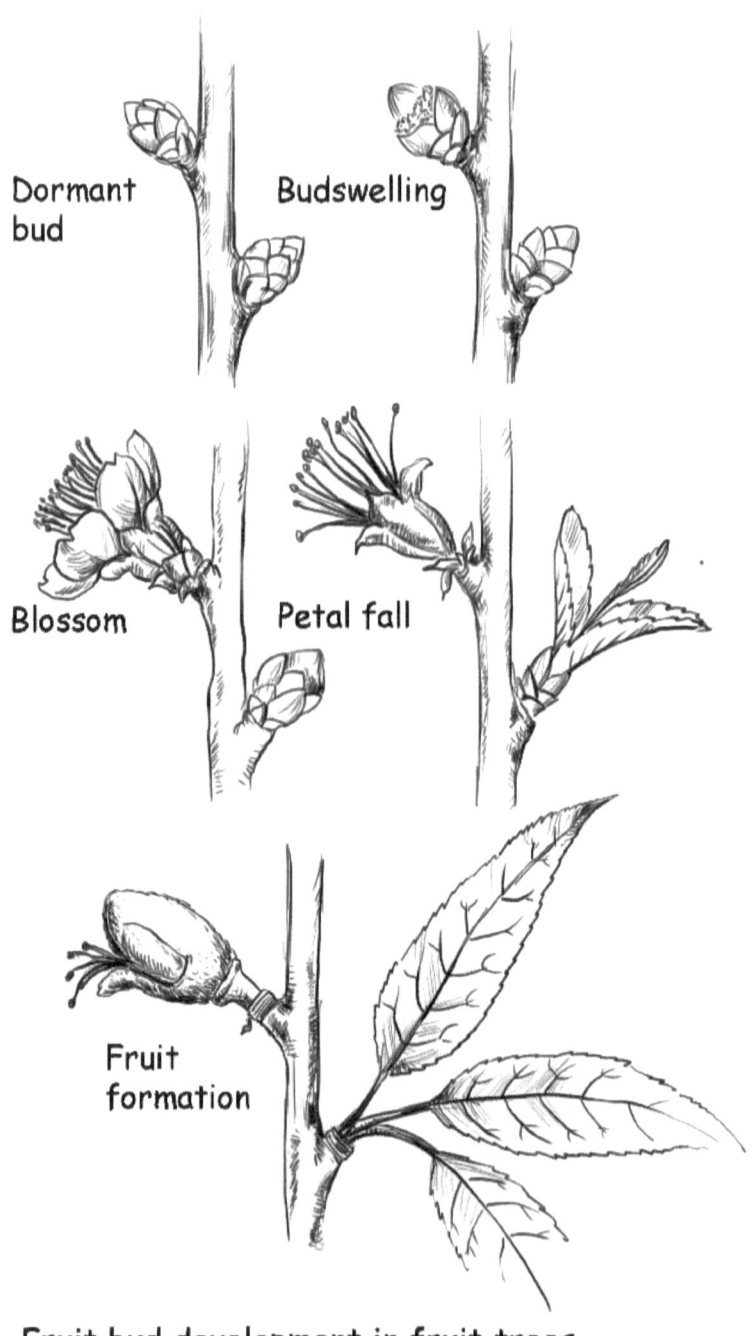

Figure 21: Stages of fruit bud development.

Time	Growth stage	Target Pests	Chemical Spray	Good to know!
Dormant	Before buds show any activity in late winter. When daytime temperatures reach 40 – 45 F. Finish spraying by noon to insure good dry time.	PEAR: overwintering scales, aphids and mites	Superior type **horticultural dormant oil Products** available under a variety of labels. Follow directions on label carefully to avoid plant damage. U.R. rate of 92% or more.	Manage pests as they hatch in early spring.
Delayed Dormant	In late winter, just as buds begin to show first green tissue. When daytime temperature is between 45 – 55 F, with no frost forecast overnight. Finish spraying by noon to insure good dry time.	APPLE & PEAR: overwintering scales, aphids, Scab, powdery mildew, rust, mites, aphids, leafrollers	Superior type horticultural dormant oil. (Oils are not effective against woolly apple aphids)	This is the most important stages and chemical spray for pest control
Pre – Pink to Petal Fall	Just before bud clusters show any color through petal fall	Powdery mildew control	Summer Horticulture Oil, Lime sulfur (Ex. Bonide Lime Sulfur)	Do not use Summer Horticulture Oil if using lime sulfur at any time of year. Do not apply lime sulfur spray to Delicious apple or Anjou pear varieties at this time as severe fruit drop can occur later. Make sure spray covers top and bottom of leaves.
		Hatching insect pests such as **mealybug, lygus bug, stinkbug, aphid, mites**	Insecticidal soaps (Safer) Cultivate beneficial insects	
		Feeding caterpillars	Spinosad (Ex. Monterey Garden Insect Spray) Bacillus thuringiensis (Ex Fertilome Dipel Pro)	
Bloom	When flowers are open.		Avoid pesticide application during bloom to protect honeybees!	
Late Spring & Early Summer	Starting 17–21 days after full bloom. Keep protected through August/mid-September.	Codling moth "Stings"- shallow entries made on surface of fruit. Treat "stung" apples as source of codling moth by removing infested apples from the tree, seal in black garbage bags. Leave in sun for two weeks to kill worms.	Start preventative spraying of fruit 17–21 days after full bloom or 10 days after petal fall. Spinosad (Ex. Monterey Garden Insect Spray) Alternative Method: Exclusion bags – these bags are placed on each fruit just after petal fall to exclude codling moth and apple maggot. This method works best on small trees. (Can be found at orchard supply stores)	**SPRAY TIMING IS CRITICAL** – First generation lasts 6 weeks, second generation lives another 6 weeks. Protect during this entire period. Follow spray schedule on label. If the apple is not protected, the eggs laid by the codling moth will hatch and the worm will enter the apple and be protected from the sprays.
	Reapply after brief, heavy rainfall or showers of longer duration, then resume regular schedule.	Apple maggot	Spinosad (Ex. Monterey Garden Insect Spray) Alternative Method: Exclusion bags	
Postharvest			REMOVE ALL FRUIT - on the tree and ground.	To reduce infestation and spread of pests to commercial orchards
Additional Information	Read the product label directions carefully. Read and follow all label directions for responsible use of any pesticide. Pesticide resistance – Vary products during the season and in following seasons to minimize pest resistance. Aphids – Seldom build up to damaging levels in home garden fruit trees. Wash them off with stream of water from the hose, you rarely have to spray.			

Compiled by: Paula Dinius, Urban Horticulturist, WSU Chelan County Extension. Revised 05/2013.

Chart 6: When to Spray Your Apple and Pear Trees

	Sour and Sweet Cherry	Peach	Plum
Fall or early spring		Pach Leaf curl	
Pink blossom buds		Captan only	
Petal fall	Curculio Leaf spot Brown rot	Tarnished plant bug Brown rot	Brown rot (fungicide only)
Shuck Splitting	Curculio Cherry maggot Brown rot	Plant bugs Curculio Brown rot	Curculio Leaf spot Brown rot
Early June	Leaf spot	Plant bugs Curculio Brown rot Scab	Curculio Leaf spot
Cherries turning color (mid June)	Maggot Leaf spot Brown rot	Plant bugs	Curculio Leaf spot Plant bugs
Early July		Pach tree borers	Leafhoppers Plant bugs Mites
After Cherry harvest time	Leaf spot Mites		
August - Spetember		Peach tree borers Brown rot	Brown rot (21-10 days before ripening)
Ripe fruits		Spottend wings drosophila	Spottend wings drosophila

Home Fruit Spray Schedule Pest Fact Sheet: Dr. Alan T. Eaton, Extension Specialist, Entomology Dr. Cheryl A. Smith, Extension Professor/Specialist, Plant Health

Chart 7 When to Spray Your Cherry, Peach, and Plum Trees

Protect Your Orchard from Uninvited Guests

Depending on your location, you may have to deal with different wildlife in addition to pests and insects. If you've got deer, squirrels, crows, or blue jays roaming around your area, then you may have to take steps to protect your harvest. Fencing could keep out the big animals such as deer. Using tree guards can prevent damage from rodents such as mice, rabbits or voles.

Birds may help chow down a number of flying insects that may harm your trees, but not all bird species flocking to your orchard are good news. Eastern bluebirds feast on snails, caterpillars, grubs, moths, and insect larvae. Swallows have a similar diet and help keep pest populations in control in the garden. Red breasted blackbirds on the other hand have a varied diet and enjoy pecking berries and fruits. To protect ripe fruits from hungry birds, you can use exclusion netting to cover the trees, shrubs, and bushes. Tying netting bags around fruit clusters is also a great way to keep them intact till harvest.

DIY Fence

Deer can be a real nuisance for young fruit trees. They'll nibble on green tender leaves, and young branches, and even rub their antlers against the trunk. The most effective way to protect your trees from deer is to install a fence or cage around your fruit trees. With a few supplies, you can create a DIY fence to ward off big animals.

Materials Required

- 5 ft x 150 ft roll of concrete wire or steel mesh
- T-Posts
- Stakes or landscape fabric staples
- Baling wire or zip ties

Directions

1. Unroll the wire around 13 ft in length and cut it.
2. Cut enough wire to fold over the t-post.
3. Fix the T-post at a distance of 3.4 to 4 ft from the tree.
4. Erect the cut pieces of wire and secure one end to the T-post with wire or zip ties.
5. Encircle the tree with the wire, making a cage-like structure by bringing the other end to the other side of the T-post.
6. Bend the long wire tabs on the T-post to secure it in place.
7. Fix tent stakes or landscape fabric staples to the bottom of the wire cage.
8. Add a second T-post for extra protection in windy locations.

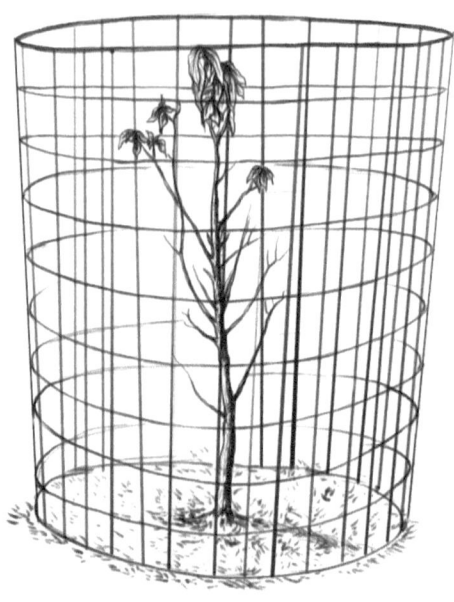

Figure 22: DIY deer fence.

The Takeaway

Running into problems in the garden is inevitable, but with the right mindset and care you can restore your trees back to health. As you begin your fruit gardening journey, you'll realize that most problems tend to resolve on their own with minimal intervention. However, if a particular disease persists, you should move gradually from the least-toxic to mildly toxic options. Pruning away the affected parts will be your best bet in most cases.

If you're tempted to use pesticides, remember that there are several non-toxic varieties available. Using biological controls such as encouraging beneficial insects can prevent a variety of diseases in the long run. Moreover, you can use various organic treatments for commonly occuring garden pests. Building fences, using tree guards, and netting can protect your harvest from deer, rodents, and birds.

Now that we've acclimatized ourselves with our enemies, let's take a look at the wonderful world of permaculture and what it has to offer. In Chapter 6, we'll discuss the role of permaculture in designing regenerative food forests.

CHAPTER 6

Enhance Garden Productivity

Now that you have a good grip on the basics, let's take things a step further. In this chapter, we'll discuss advanced strategies to reap maximum benefits from your home orchard. So without further ado, let's jump right into techniques to upgrade your gardening game.

Permaculture

If you've read my previous two books, then you're no stranger to permaculture and its multitude of benefits. If this is the first time you're encountering this term, then here's a quick lowdown about what it means. Permaculture is a system of design that strives to fulfill human needs without compromising the environment. In simple words, it encourages food growers to work in harmony with existing ecosystems on their land. It includes practices commonly observed in nature such as no waste and closed loop systems.

Bill Mollison, an Australian researcher, coined the term in 1978. It is a contraction of the words 'permanent agriculture' and 'permanent culture'. As the name implies, permaculture aims to create a sustainable form of living. It strives to create agricultural ecosystems that are diverse, stable, resilient and in harmony with nature.

The cornerstone of permaculture is to work with, not against nature. This can only be achieved through thoughtful observation instead of thoughtless action. For example, by observing your land, you can learn how different systems interact with each other. This allows you to find creative solutions to your problems that benefit existing ecosystems and help you achieve your goals.

I've discussed permaculture and its principles in detail in my first book, *The Practical Permaculture Project*. If you want to learn more about permaculture and its applications, be sure to check it out. The techniques we'll be discussing in this chapter are all based on permaculture. As you'll see below, living in harmony with your environment is the linchpin of effective gardening.

Companion Planting

Plants, like people, thrive when they're surrounded by friends. Companion planting involves growing various crops near one another to improve crop production. Grouping mutually beneficial plants with each other maximizes the benefits. Meanwhile, planting the same species together may lead to increased infestations of pests or disease.

Companion planting not only proves beneficial for plants but also helps maximize space. Additionally, it deters harmful insects, provides shade to smaller plants, suppresses weeds, draws beneficial insects, and increases soil health. One of the most famous companion plantings, 'The Three Sisters,' involves growing beans, squash, and corn together. Corn, the taller plant, behaves as a natural support trellis. It provides shelter for the two climbing plants peas and beans, which in turn enrich the soil with nitrogen. Lastly, squash and pumpkin provide shade to the smaller pea and bean plants as well as suppress weeds. There are plenty of benefits for companion planting with fruit trees too.

Options for fruit tree companions:

Queen Anne's Lace, Bergamot, Coriander, Thyme, Borage, Zinnia, Parsley, Cosmos, Dill, Sunflowers, Alyssum, Mint, Fennel, Phaecelia (purple tansy).

Just as grouping compatible plants improves harvest, pairing incompatible species can lead to more problems. For example, growing onions and beans together could stunt the growth of the beans.

The Clover Solution

Let's take a moment to picture a flourishing orchard with a green carpet of clover covering the ground. Not only do these fields of clover increase the orchard's beauty, they also play a significant role in establishing a thriving ecosystem. Including clover as a cover crop boosts the health of your fruit trees while attracting a host of pollinators.

Here are some reasons why you should be planting lucky clovers in your backyard orchard.

1. **Boosted Pollination:** They foster biodiversity by drawing a host of beneficial insects such as bees, butterflies, and various other pollinators. They serve as an additional food source for pollinator populations, improving pollination and increasing fruit yield. A burgeoning pollinator population restores balance to the ecosystem.

2. **Nitrogen Fixation:** Clovers, especially legume varieties such as red or white clover, possess excellent nitrogen-fixation characteristics. This reduces the need for synthetic fertilizers, minimizing environmental pollution and decreasing the overall cost. The nitrogen-enriched soil enhances garden productivity, resulting in a bountiful harvest.

3. **Weed Suppression:** The dense clover growth sprouting at your feet acts as a weed-suppressing blanket. They restrict the

growth of unwanted weeds by competing for the same resources. The four-leafed clovers block sunlight from reaching the soil, minimizing the need for herbicides, and contributing to a more sustainable ecosystem.

4. **Prevent Soil Erosion:** Their sprawling root systems cling to the soil particles, holding them together and preventing erosion. This helps protect the topsoil from getting washed away during rainfall.

5. **Moisture Retention:** The multitude of clovers sprouting from the ground help conserve soil moisture. By preventing direct sunlight from reaching the soil surface, they behave as mulch by slowing down evaporation. Improving the soil's moisture retention ability, reduces water stress for orchard trees during dry spells.

6. **Aesthetics:** In addition to its functional benefits, it enhances the visual appeal of the orchard. The vibrant green field of clover serves as a breathtaking backdrop for fruit-bearing trees. Moreover, it minimizes the risks of soil compaction and erosion due to foot traffic or heavy machinery.

Guilding

Guilding is an effective technique to level up your gardening game. Guilds are unlike monocultures such as corn fields or apple orchards. Based on the principle of companion planting, they include diverse plant, insect, and animal species living together in a mini ecosystem. The focal point of these systems is a primary food source such as an apple tree. Figure 22 illustrates the different layers of an edible food forest including the canopy, the sub canopy, and the ground cover.

1. Canopy/Tall Tree
2. Sub-Canopy/Large Shrub
3. Shrub
4. Herbaceous
5. Ground Cover/Creeper
6. Underground
7. Vertical/Climber

Figure 22: Different layers of an edible forest garden.

Benefits of Guilding

Bunching up compatible systems works wonders. It's a win-win for all the plant and animal species involved, but why is it so? What makes tree guilds so effective in maximizing productivity? Let's find out what guilding looks like and why you shouldn't be missing out on its enormous benefits.

At the heart of a guild is a fruit tree. The plants chosen are usually found growing together in nature and perform multiple functions. Underplantings may include plants that fertilize the soil, ward off pests, attract pollinators, suppress weeds, and create mulch. Taking the advantage of grouping multiple plants can help reduce the overall cost and labor involved.

For example, coupling nitrogen fixing plants with species that produce potassium, calcium, phosphorus, and other minerals can improve soil nutritional content. Moreover, utilizing natural food webs helps recycle plant debris, creating healthy soil with excellent moisture retention abilities. Planting insectary plants can draw beneficial insect predators such as lacewings, ladybugs, and wasps as well as native bees. This can help keep pest populations in check while increasing harvest.

Aromatic plants such as garlic, thyme, oregano, and yarrow ward off pests. Meanwhile, dense layers of herbs and groundcover plants prevent weeds and protect the soil. A diverse collection of plants attracts a wide range of fungi, bacteria, insects, and birds, further strengthening the ecosystem. Allowing natural processes to take place unhindered, reduces overall workload in the garden. Pairing the right plants can make watering more efficient, suppress weed populations, prevent soil erosion, and shield sensitive varieties from sunscald and harsh winds.

Choosing the right plants may seem like an exhaustive process, which is why I compiled the list below. In the next chart you'll find the names of various plants and the functions they perform within fruit guilds.

1. CanopyLayer	Black Cherry, Chestnut, Lime, Hazelnut, Mulberry, OsageOrange, Pecan, Persimmon, Walnut
2. Sub-Canopy	Apple, Sweet Cherry, Tart Cherry, Hazelnut, Jujube, PawPaw, AsianPears, Plum, Quince, Serviceberry
3. ShrubLayer	Aronia, Blueberries, Sweet Cherry, Tart Cherry, Chestnut, GojiBerry, Hazelnut, OsageOrange, Rosemary, Roses, Sage
4. HerbaceousLayer	Asparagus, Buckwheat, Red Clover, Echinacea, Fennel, Oregano, Parsley, Rhubarb, Plantain, Sorrel, Yarrow

5. GroundCovers	Red Clover, Calendula, CreepingBlueberry, Mint, Oregano, GroundRaspberry, Sage, Strawberries, Sweet Potato
6. Underground	Carrots, Ginseng, Groundnut, Horseradish, Parsley, Radishes, Turnips, Sweet Potato
7. Vines / Climbing	Cucumber, HogPeanut, Hops, Kiwi, PassionFruit, PeaVines, Sweet Potato, Grapes
8. WetlandLayer	Common Reed, WaterLotus, Willow, WaterSpinach, Watercress, WaterChestnuts
9. FungalLayer	Reishi/Ling Chi, ShaggyMane, Shiitake

Table 2: .Species and functions

Fruit Tree Guilds: A Blueprint

The possibilities are endless. Take your pick of trees from the vast array, pair those with similar characteristics and enjoy a multitude of benefits. So, how do you go about reaping the enormous benefits of this ingenious gardening technique? As always, let's start with the basics: what to plant and how to plant it.

What to Choose?

Heirloom, disease-resistant, or genetically diverse plants are all great options for stress- and hassle-free gardening. They're healthy and resilient, cutting your workload in half. Some growers might opt for rare varieties that can't be easily purchased at markets or grocery stores. These may include heirloom apples, pawpaw, jujube, persimmon, Saskatoon berry, mulberry, or nuts such as chestnuts.

A Step-by-Step Guide

The first steps to establish fruit guilds require some heavy lifting. However, a little effort in the beginning will eventually pay off in the form of a flourishing garden. Here is a step-by-step guide to fruit guilding:

1. **Berms:** Constructing berms can significantly increase soil fertility. Start by cutting grass and building circular terraces or mounds that are 3 x 3 meters in diameter. This can also help if your ground soil is composed of heavy clay.

2. **Lasagna Beds:** Making lasagna beds is also an effective way to boost soil fertility. It involves placing layers of organic matter on the soil that decompose over time, creating a fertile garden bed.

3. **Mulch Basins:** Digging mulch bains reduces water requirements by storing rain or greywater. A moat, 25 - 45 cm deep around the perimeter of the garden with a berm can collect rainwater, fulfilling the garden's watering requirements.

4. **Shift Soil:** Fungal mycorrhizae are essential for fruit trees' nutritional needs. Before guilding, you can shift the soil toward fungal dominance by removing grasses and weeds and introducing wood chips and native soil from the area around mature apple trees.

5. **Plant trees:** Start by creating a mound with the soil displaced while digging the hole. Stake the tree if required and position a graft knob facing north to shield the graft with the tree's shade.

6. **The Perfect Mix:** Select eight or nine supporting plant species. These should vary in size. Ideally, one small, one medium, and one large. Additionally, there should be a small nitrogen fixing tree, a small shrub, one or two ground cover crops, and four or five herbaceous perennials.

The supporting plants should be treated as sacrificial. As the nitrogen fixing plants grow too big, you may cut them out. Smaller species may die out as the sunlight fails to reach them once larger plants grow more dense. All this is part of the cycle.

There are no limits to what you can accomplish through fruit guilding. Thinking strategically in the beginning can help overcome future obstacles. Planting shrubs such as berry bushes or nitrogen-fixing shrubs in the southwest can help protect against winter sunscald.

Apple Tree Guild

An apple tree guild is an excellent example of fruit tree guilds. Planting daffodils and garlic chives around the tree helps prevent wild grasses from creeping in and repels wildlife. Planting bee balm, fennel, and dill underneath the first layer attracts pollinators.

A third layer of comfrey, yarrow, dandelion, and white clover helps accumulate nutrients and fix nitrogen thereby enriching the soil. Comfrey and nasturtiums are also great for providing mulch or green manure. Meanwhile, the strong scents of bee balm, yarrow, and garlic chives repel a multitude of pests. Fennel and garlic chives also impart anti-fungal properties to apple trees, which are prone to scab fungus.

Once you've mastered the art of fruit guilding, perhaps you could move onto more complex structures such as a food forest. The set up contains diverse plant species mimicking the ecosystems and patterns found in nature. Food forests have a three-dimensional design. Life extends in all directions: upward, downward, and outward.

A food forest or forest garden generally has seven layers: the understory, the overstory, the herbaceous layer, the shrub layer, the ground cover, the vine layer, and the root layer. Some permaculturists also like to add an eighth layer, the mycelial layer, consisting of mushrooms. The food forest design allows us to grow more plants in a limited area without having them competing with each other. Figure

23 illustrates a food forest with a combination of fruit trees, grasses, ground cover plants, and climbers.

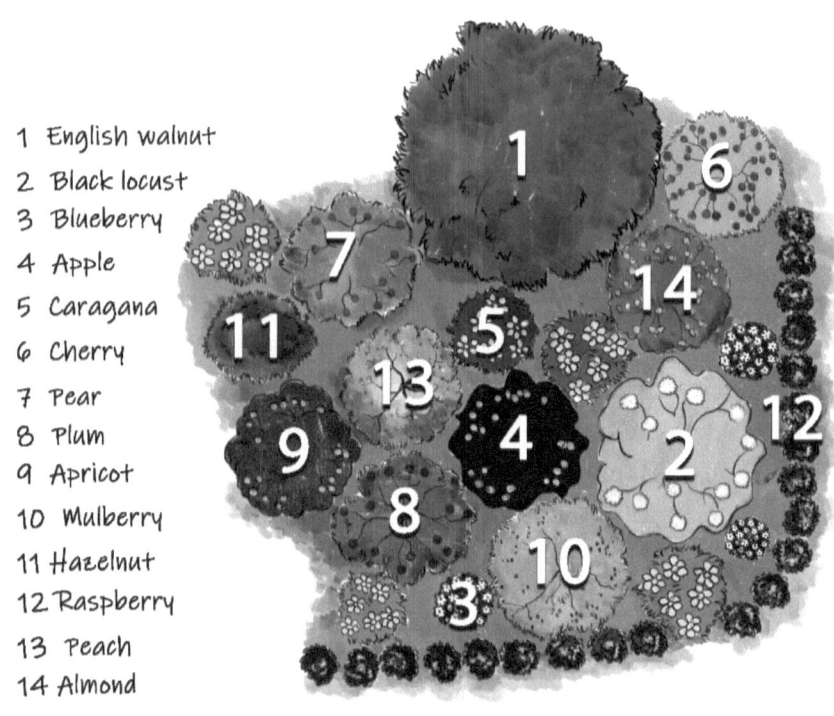

1 English walnut
2 Black locust
3 Blueberry
4 Apple
5 Caragana
6 Cherry
7 Pear
8 Plum
9 Apricot
10 Mulberry
11 Hazelnut
12 Raspberry
13 Peach
14 Almond

Figure 23: Food forest

The Year-Round Harvest

Imagine going into the nursery and picking out your favorite fruit trees, only to find them all ripening at the same time a few weeks later. You'll not only have trouble harvesting, you'll have nothing left for the rest of the year, not to mention that most of the fruits harvested will go to waste.

Successive ripening involves strategically choosing varieties that ripen one after the other, ensuring an uninterrupted supply of delicious fresh fruits. It's best to plant fruit varieties with overlapping harvest seasons ranging from earliest to latest. Choose fruit trees with the ripening time in mind. Here are a few examples:

Ten Months of Juicy Oranges

Here's how you can ensure a continuous supply of tangy, juicy oranges. Choose early-season Cara Cara Oranges, midseason ripening Washington Navel, and late-season Valencia. You'll have an abundant supply of homegrown oranges from three trees that last over ten months.

Eight Months of Mandarins

Plant early-season Owari Satsuma Mandarin, mid-season Gold Nugget Mandarin, and late-season Pixie Mandarin. For the next eight months, you'll have an abundant supply of fresh, tree-ripe mandarins!

Five Months of Delicious Apples

Choose a widely adapted, early-season Gravenstein Apple, mid-season Gala, and late-season Fuji for four months of delicious apples. Add a late season Granny Smith for your pies and cobblers and you can enjoy five months of fresh apple harvest!

In the chart below, I've compiled different fruit varieties and their harvest times. The list will give you an idea about which varieties you should plant.

Cherries	APR	MAY	JUN	JUL	AUG	SEP	OCT	NOV	DEC
Craig's Crimson – Early May to June		x	x						
Royal Rainier – mid May to mid June		x	x						
Lapins – June to late June			x	x					

Apples	APR	MAY	JUN	JUL	AUG	SEP	OCT	NOV	DEC
Dorsett Golden – July through August				x	x	x			
Fuji – August through October					x	x	x		
Granny Smith – October through January							x	x	x
Gala – August through September					x	x			
Pettingill – September through October						x	x		
Pink Lady – October through December							x	x	x

Pears - European	APR	MAY	JUN	JUL	AUG	SEP	OCT	NOV	DEC
Hood – mid July to mid August				x	x				
Flordahome – late July through August				x	x				
Seckel – mid August to mid September									
Kieffer – September through mid October									

Pears - Asian	APR	MAY	JUN	JUL	AUG	SEP	OCT	NOV	DEC
Shinseiki – mid July to mid August				x	x				
Hosui – August					x				
TsuLi and YaLi – August through September					x	x			
Shinko – September						x			

Apricots	APR	MAY	JUN	JUL	AUG	SEP	OCT	NOV	DEC
Royal Rosa Apricot – early May to June		x	x						
Blenheim Apricot – mid June to early July			x	x					
Tomcot – late May to mid June		x	x						
Nugget – mid June to early July			x	x					
Canadian White Blenheim – late June to mid July			x	x					
EarliAutumn – late July to late August				x	x				

Peaches - White	APR	MAY	JUN	JUL	AUG	SEP	OCT	NOV	DEC
TropicSnow – early June to July			x	x					
Donut – late June to mid July			x	x					
Babcock – early to late July				x					

Dave Wilson Nursery / Tom Spellman: In The Backyard Orchard Culture Style, 2023

Peaches - Yellow	APR	MAY	JUN	JUL	AUG	SEP	OCT	NO
May Pride – May		x						
Eva'sPride – June			x					
Mid Pride – July				x				
August Pride – August					x			

Peaches - DoubleFlowering / Fruiting	APR	MAY	JUN	JUL	AUG	SEP	OCT	NO
DoubleJewel – mid June to early July			x	x				
Red Baron – late June to mid July			x	x				
Saturn – mid July to early August				x	x			

Nectarines - White	APR	MAY	JUN	JUL	AUG	SEP	OCT	NO
Arctic Star – mid June,			x					
ArcticGlo – late June early July			x	x				
Arctic Rose – mid to late July				x				
ArcticQueen – early to mid August					x			

Nectarines - Yellow	APR	MAY	JUN	JUL	AUG	SEP	OCT	NO
DesertDelight – early to late June			x					
DoubleDelight – early to mid July				x				
Panamint – late July to early August				x	x			
ZeeGlo – mid to late August					x			

Plums - Japanese	APR	MAY	JUN	JUL	AUG	SEP	OCT	NO
Methley – June			x					
Shiro – late June to mid July			x	x				
Catalina – mid July to mid August				x	x			
Golden Nectar – mid August to early September					x	x		
Beauty - June			x					
Santa Rosa – early to mid July				x				
Burgundy – July to late August				x	x			
EmeraldBeaut – late August to mid October					x	x	x	

Persimmons: Fuyu, Hachiya, Chocolate and CoffeeCake (NishimuraWase) – September through December

Blueberries: Misty, O'Neal, and Sharpblue – Blueberries will ripen periodically throughout the spring and Although considered self-fruitful, planting three or more varieties together will insure bumper crops.

Chart 8: Different fruit varieties and their harvest times

Maximize Your Space: Grow in Containers

What if you don't have a sizable portion of land to work with? What if you live in an apartment or a small home? Does it mean you should miss out on the joys of fruit gardening? If you're short on space, you can grow fruits in containers. Whether you live in an apartment or simply have a small patio to work with, you can create a mini-orchard by growing fruit trees in pots.

Here's everything you need to know about planting trees in pots.

How to Grow Fruit Trees in Pots

The process begins with choosing the right container. A 10-15 gallon pot is generally considered suitable for supporting a tree. The size is small enough to be moved with ease. A container of this size can be easily placed on a window, a balcony, or patio. It can also be relocated indoors when the weather gets too cold.

Containers are excellent for warm-weather varieties such as banana, fig, and citrus trees, especially if you live in a cool climate. It's best to start small, with a five- or seven-gallon pot. As the tree matures, it'll become root-bound and stop growing. It'll still keep producing leaves and fruits; however, you may want to start looking for a bigger container.

It's important to keep in mind that without adequate drainage, your tree won't keep growing for very long. Holes at the bottom or the sides of the containers drain excess water while allowing the soil access to air. This reduces the potential of root rot.

Using the right soil is also crucial to the success of containerized fruit trees. Potting soil is mostly considered the best option as it is especially formulated for container planting. Top soil should be avoided as it can become compacted, which may lead to more watering issues.

Prepare your containers by adding a first layer of gravel or rock to enhance drainage. Add some of your potting mix on top and place your tree in the center. Add the remaining soil and press with your hands to remove air pockets. Give it a thorough watering and you're on your way to creating your mini orchard!

Let's look at some of the steps outlined above in more detail, so you can make the best decision for your plants.

Choosing Containers

Container material ranges from terracotta, metal, wood, and plastic. While each has its own characteristics, your decision should be based on what suits your tree's requirements and your budget. The considerations you should bear in mind are the size of your container and its ability to bear the weight of the tree, offer moisture retention and good drainage.

Metal containers usually have poor drainage and tend to heat up quickly when placed in sunlight. Terracotta provides good drainage and water retention, but tends to break easily. Plastic pots are cheap but may not be able to bear the weight of the wet soil and a top-heavy tree. In the end, you should make your decision after weighing the pros and cons of various container materials.

Selecting the Right Soil

Fruit trees thrive in loam-based compost that is fairly heavy, providing great stability. Before filling the pots with soil, line the container with broken pieces of terracotta or a few rocks to improve drainage.

Aftercare

Trees growing in containers will dry out faster than the ones planted in the ground. Regular watering is required for potted trees to fulfill daily moisture needs. However, it's important to keep the compost moist, but not wet.

You can use a simple testing kit to measure the soil's pH and adjust according to your trees' requirements. Give your trees a boost each spring by refreshing the top layer of compost. Start by scraping away about 5 cm (2 inches) of compost from the top and sprinkle fresh compost mixed with controlled release fertilizer granules. During winter, use hessian or bubble wrap to wrap the containers. This will protect the roots from the freezing temperatures.

Fruits Best Suited for Containers (Dwarf Varieties)

Here are a list of fruits that are best suited for growing in containers:

- Apple
- Apricot
- Cherry
- Fig
- Lemon
- Orange
- Peach
- Pear
- Plum

Grafting

Why go through the trouble of growing 40 different fruit trees when you can have 40 different fruit varieties from a single tree? The tree in question is found in California and is referred to as the "Tree of 40 Fruits." Created by Sam Van Aken, this incredible tree has plums growing on one branch, apricots and peaches others. Forty different varieties of stone fruits can be found growing on the tree. This is the marvel of grafting.

Grafting is the practice of fusing two trees into one. To achieve this, you need a rootstock and scion. The lower part, the rootstock, will form the roots of the new fruit tree. It controls how tall the tree will grow. The scion, the upper portion of the graft, determines the fruit type, flavor, and color.

Fruit trees are not usually grown directly from seeds. Rather they're cross-pollinated to create the best tasting varieties. The resulting tree possesses entirely new genetic makeup that is a mixture of the parent trees. Grafted fruit trees offer the following benefits:

- They offer pest and disease resistance.
- They can be designed to withstand cold climates.
- They can be used to produce dwarf or semi-dwarf varieties.

On the other hand, fruit trees grown from seeds present significant disadvantages. For example, the fruit they produce is small and sour. They can grow to massive sizes, which can be difficult to manage, and they may take several years to produce fruits. Without grafting, we wouldn't have some famous fruit varieties we see today, such as the Macintosh apple trees.

How Does It Work?

If you make a cut into a young tree branch, you may notice that it has a brown bark, but green inner tissue known as the cambium. This is an essential part of the tree, providing continual growth and renewal.

Without a cambium, grafting can't be done. To graft a fruit tree, you'll need to make a cut on your scion and another on the rootstock. The next step is to bind these two parts together. The wound on both parts sends signals to the plant to repair the damage. As the wound heals, the two trees become secured together.

A Guide to Grafting Fruit Trees

1. **Gather scionwood** during the winter, when the plant is dormant and requires less energy. Make sure the scionwood is healthy, by inspecting it for any abnormalities. Take a 16-inch

cutting. Label the tree's name and the date the cutting was taken. The scion wood should be a year old with about three leaf buds pointing upward.

2. **Choose botanically compatible scion and rootstocks.** Many fruit varieties can only be grafted on tree parts from the same species, such as apples. Others, such as apricots, are more flexible. Similarly, plums can be grafted onto an almond rootstock. Compatibility is largely influenced by genetic relatedness as well as similar physical characteristics. For example, almost all citrus varieties can be grafted onto each other. Cherries, plums, and apples go well together. Rootstock of European pear is compatible with Asian pear in addition other European pear varieties. Peaches can be grafted on other peach varieties as well as nectarines, European plums, and apricots. Quince respond well to other quince varieties, pear, and loquat.

3. **Store the cutting** in the fridge by wrapping it in a damp paper towel and placing it in a plastic bag. Keep it there until spring to maintain dormancy. Make sure to keep a check and remove any ripened fruit so the accumulated ethylene doesn't damage the scionwood.

4. **Begin grafting** in the spring. Check the trees in your neighborhood to see if any buds are beginning to open. This can give you an indication that the sap is starting to flow, making it the perfect time for grafting.

5. **Seal** the scion and graft union to prevent dehydration and bind it to ensure the cambia of the two parts remain in contact.

6. **Ensure cross-pollination** by grafting or planting two varieties.

Grafting Techniques

There are various grafting techniques that you can choose from depending on what you're looking to achieve. If your intention is to make an old tree productive then bark grafting might be a suitable option for you. Based on your timing and preference, the whip and tongue method or bud grafting may offer an effective solution. Let's look at each method in more detail.

Bark Grafting

Through this method, you can renew old fruit trees. Through bark grafting you can improve the quality of old fruit trees. For this method, you must peel the bark with a sharp knife, exposing the cambium, and insert the scion. Secure both parts by tying them together with some elastic bands.

Figure 24 illustrates the method of bark grafting, especially for thick-barked trees. In such cases, the vertical cut of the bark is unnecessary. The scion is instead inserted between the bark and wood of the stock.

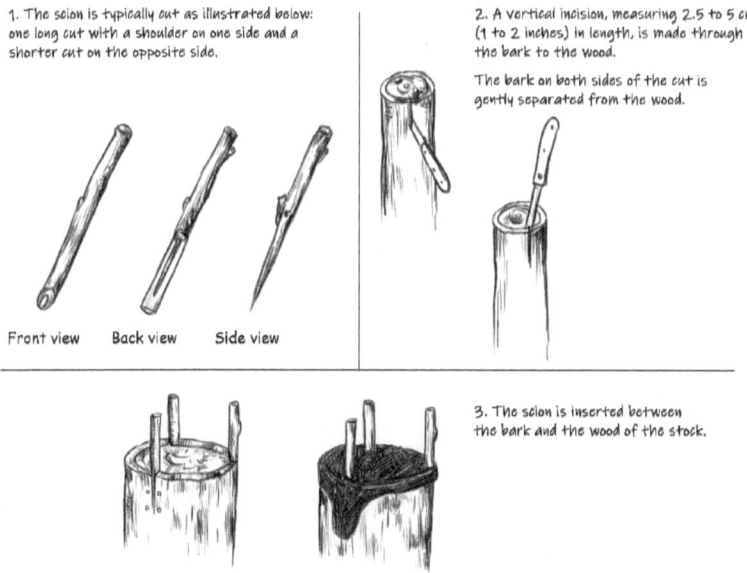

Figure 24: Bark grafting.

Whip and Tongue Technique

It works exactly like a jigsaw puzzle. You make a long, slanting cut. This will provide the maximum surface area between the rootstock and the scion. You'll need a sharp knife, some wax and elastic bands. Figure 25 below illustrates the whip and tongue method.

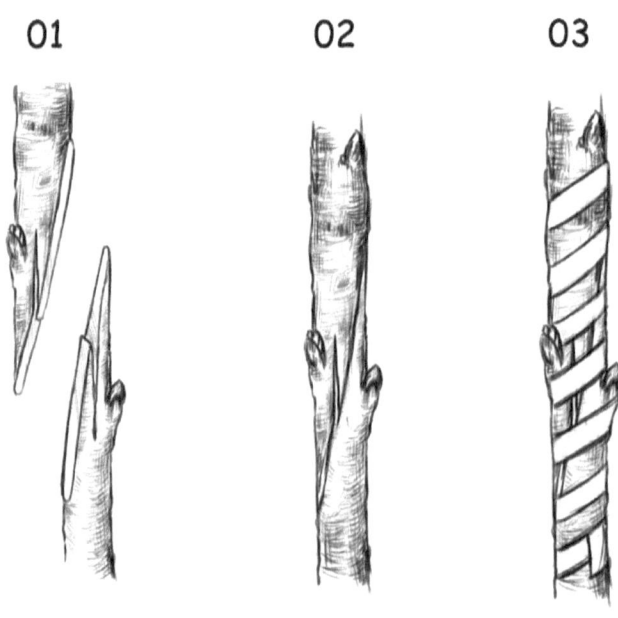

Whip and Tongue grafting

Figure 25: Whip and tongue grafting method.

Top-Wedge Technique

The technique involves using a wedge-shaped cut to combine the scion and the rootstock. Usually, this grafting method is performed during the tree dormancy. Start by selecting a healthy scion and a compatible rootstock. With a sharp grafting knife, make diagonal cuts on both plants, making a wedge shape. Fix the wedge-shaped scion into the rootstock and secure the graft with grafting tape or rubber bands. Make sure the cambium layers of both the scion and the rootstock are in close contact.

You can also use grafting wax or any other similar material to prevent the union from drying out. Cover the graft with a plastic bag to retain moisture and promote healing. Check regularly for signs of growth and remove the covering when the graft is established.

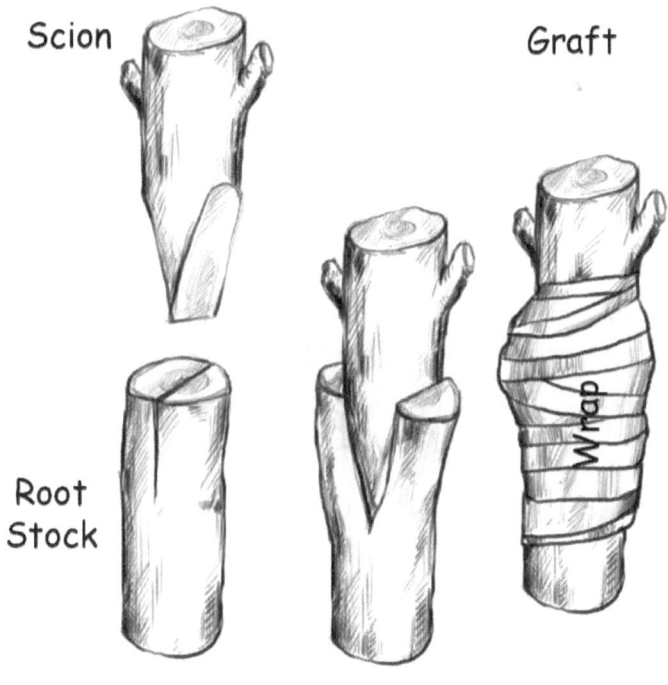

Figure 26: Top wedge grafting.

Bud Grafting

If you missed the early season for grafting, you can graft your fruit using a different technique. Simply take a single bud from the desired scion. Make a T-cut or a chip cut on your rootstock and insert the bud.

The Takeaway

We discussed the various ways through which we can enhance garden productivity. Using permaculture principles while designing our backyard orchards allows us to make the most of our resources without inflicting damage on our environment. Companion planting is an excellent method of enriching plants by grouping compatible varieties. It helps create a self-sufficient garden. Guilding is also a great way to grow diverse plant species that benefit one another.

If limited space is an issue, we can always grow trees in containers. While not every tree is suitable for this, it gives garden lovers an opportunity to experience the joys of growing fruit trees despite having limited space. Lastly, grafting is a fantastic method to grow trees with the desired characteristics and considerably enhance garden productivity. In the next chapter, we will look at pollination and how to attract pollinators to your backyard.

CHAPTER 7

Bring the Bees to the Yard

Pollination is essential for the development of fruits. So let's talk about the birds and the bees and the flowers blooming on the fruit trees in your backyard orchard. Fruit tree pollination entails reproduction and fruit development. Without pollination, there will be no fruits to harvest. It involves the transfer of pollen from the stamen to the pistil. This leads to fertilization and the development of seeds. The honey bees and hummingbirds that may wander into your orchard are essential to making all that happen!

Based on pollination, fruit trees can be sorted into two categories:

- **Self-Pollinating:** Trees that don't require other tree varieties to achieve pollination. These include apricots, peaches, sour cherries, and peaches.

- **Cross-Pollinating:** Trees that require another tree variety for pollination. Fruit trees such as pear, plums, and sweet cherries fall in this category.

To ensure effective pollination, it's best to plant at least two compatible pollen varieties within a hundred feet of each other. Make sure that the trees you choose bloom in the same season. Timing is everything for successful pollination. Early-season trees will pollinate other early-season trees. The same principle applies to mid- or late-season varieties.

Pollination

Let's look at pollination in more detail and try to understand this fascinating phenomenon. Everything starts with a flower. Pollen grains get transferred from the male part of the blossom to the female part. Fertilization takes place in the ovary when sperm cells from the pollen grain fuse with the egg, producing seeds or embryos. Following fertilization, the ovary transforms into fruit, enclosing the seeds.

Pollinators play an important role in carrying pollen from the male to the female part of the flower. They include a long list of insects and animals. However, sometimes pollination can take place by something as simple as the wind. It is important to note that some trees require specific pollinators. For instance, almond trees depend on honey bees while cherry trees are somewhat dependent on bees to achieve pollination.

As I mentioned above, some trees' flowers are incompatible with their own pollen, requiring cross pollination instead. For example, many apple varieties are only suitable for cross-pollination.

On the other hand, persimmons exclusively require cross-pollination and the transfer of pollen from the male to the female tree. Persimmon flowers are either male or female and require a pollinator for the transfer of pollen grains. The tree that generates pollen is known as the pollenizer.

It's important to note that the fruits produced by cross pollination will be similar to the tree that received the pollen. However, the seeds will be hybrids and share characteristics of the parent plants. For instance, if a Red Delicious apple is pollinated by a Granny Smith, the resulting fruits will all be of the Red Delicious variety, but the seeds within these fruits will possess varying characteristics.

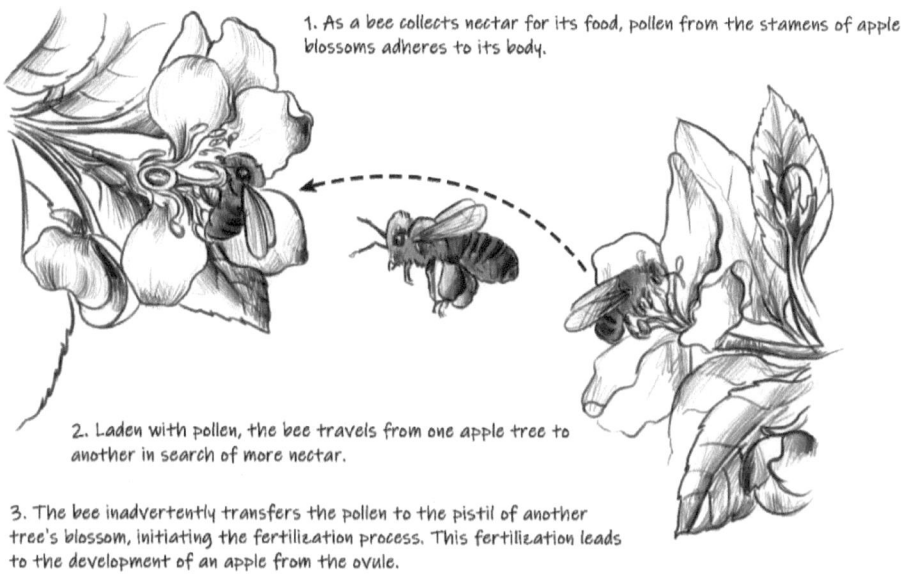

1. As a bee collects nectar for its food, pollen from the stamens of apple blossoms adheres to its body.

2. Laden with pollen, the bee travels from one apple tree to another in search of more nectar.

3. The bee inadvertently transfers the pollen to the pistil of another tree's blossom, initiating the fertilization process. This fertilization leads to the development of an apple from the ovule.

Figure 27: Bees as pollinators.

Which varieties should you plant? Which pollinators should you try to attract to your garden? If any of those questions have got you scratching your head, look no further. In Chart 9, I've compiled a list of various fruit trees, the kind of pollinators they require, and their self-pollinating varieties so you can choose what works best for you.

FRUIT TREE	POLLENIZER REQUIRED	POLLINATORS	SELF-POLLINATION VARIETIES
Apple	most varieties	insects, especially honeybees	Ein Shemer, Gala, Golden Delicious, Dorsett Golden, Anna
Banana	no	none required	All
Cherry	some varieties	insects, especially honeybees	Benton, Blackgold, Lapins, Starkrimso, Stella, Whitegold, Tart Cherries
Fig	no	none required	All
Olive	some varieties	various insects	Arbequina
Peach	some varieties	various insects	FlordaCrest
Pear	yes	insects, especially honeybees	Kieffer, Shinseiki, Gulf Crimson, Pineapple Pear
Pecan	yes	the wind	Self-pollination is minimal and generally does not produce good quality nuts.
Persimmon	yes, a male tree	insects, especially honeybees	Asian Kaki Persimmons, Fuyu
Plum	most	insects, especially honeybees	Au Rosa, Golden, Methley, Santa Rosa, Scarlet Beauty
Pomegranate	no	insects, especially honeybees	All

Chart 9: Required pollinators for fruit trees

Pros and Cons of Self and Cross Pollination

By now, you may have made up your mind which pollination type suits you best. However, before you commit yourself to buying certain types of trees, let's look at the advantages and disadvantages of both methods.

Pros of Self-Pollination

1. The specific characteristics of the tree are preserved down several generations.
2. It doesn't require pollinators.
3. There's no need to invest in methods to attract insect pollinators to your orchard.
4. It guarantees the production of seeds.
5. There's no wastage of microspores.
6. It gets rid of unwanted recessive characteristics.

Cons of Self-Pollination

1. It prevents the plants from adapting to environmental changes.
2. It may lead to weaker offsprings.
3. It may produce seeds of low quality.

Pros of Cross-Pollination

1. It produces a large number of healthy seeds.
2. It gives rise to new varieties.
3. It helps the resulting generations adapt to environmental stresses.
4. It often leads to superior quality fruit.

Cons of Cross-Pollination

1. It can be labor and cost intensive, requiring efforts to attract pollinators and plant different tree varieties.

The Who's Who of Pollinators

Pollinators are the garden's elite force. The animals and insects responsible for pollination play an undeniably important role in the success of fruit orchards. So who are these tiny crusaders and how do they operate?

The list of pollinators is a long one, including birds, bats, and a wide range of insects. Some of these you may be familiar with, such as bees and butterflies. Others, like flies, beetles, and wasps, may come as a surprise. Here's a brief overview of some of these pollinators, their habitat, lifecycles, and conservation needs.

Solitary Bees

Honey bees may just be the most widely known pollinators. Surprisingly, they make up a tiny fraction of the bee species. There are approximately 20,000 species of bees worldwide. Out of these, 3,600 bee species are native to Canada and the United States alone. The solitary bees make up the majority of non-aggressive bee species, since most of them are stingless. They possess tiny hairs and specialized anatomical structures that collect and transfer pollen.

Plants that Attract Bees: Goldenrod, borage, black-eyed Susan, lupine, liatris, bee balm, nasturtium, pansy, marigold ,poppies, zinnia, sunflower ,lavender, lupineec hinacea, phlox, mint.

Bumble Bees

Their ability to fly in cold temperatures and low light makes them one of the best pollinators, especially for people situated in high elevations and latitudes. They have round, fuzzy bodies and grasp flowers in their jaws before using their wing muscles to release the pollen.

Butterflies

Butterflies tend to be less efficient than bees at moving pollen but serve as valuable pollinators nonetheless. They pick most of the pollen on their long, slender legs, lacking specialized structures for transporting it.

Plants that attract butterflies: Milkweed, ironweed, sunflowers, violets, bee balm, snapdragon, dill, phlox, cornflower, butterfly bush, goldenrod, echinacea, mallow, blue wild indigo, lilac, daisies, sage, zinnia, Joe-Pye weeds

Moths

As the night sets in, moths take over pollination duty from the bees and butterflies. They are an incredibly diverse group of insects, with various moth species adapted to pollinating a large array of plants. Some moths feed exclusively on night-blooming flowers for nectar while others are important pollinators for fruit trees such as pears, plums, and apples.

Plants that attract moths include: Fireweed, moonflower, four o'clocks, honeysuckle, salvia, monarda, foxglove, heliotrope.

Wasps

Wasps often receive unjust criticism for their perceived aggressiveness. In reality, they are highly skilled hunters, and we should appreciate their valuable ecological roles. They make significant contributions to our environment by helping to maintain insect populations, managing pests, and serving as essential participants in conservation and biological control efforts. Interestingly, when we consider their evolutionary origins, bees can be viewed essentially as vegetarian wasps!

Many wasp species have smooth bodies and do not actively collect pollen. Unlike bees, they lack the branched, pollen-trapping hairs typically associated with bee pollination. Consequently, they play a relatively minor role in the pollination of most plants. However, they do inadvertently aid in pollination by transporting and dispersing some pollen grains as they move between flowers.

Plants that attract wasps include: Yarrow, cool-colored flowers (blue, white, purple), lemongrass, parsley, mint, marigold, lemon balm, ferns, moss.

Flies

Comprising an astounding array of over eighty-five-thousand species across the globe, flies represent one of the most diverse insect orders, known as Diptera. While certain fly species are often associated with being agricultural pests and vectors of disease, it's crucial to recognize that many play vital and beneficial roles in ecosystems. This includes aquatic midges, which serve as a plentiful food source for migratory birds, and the fly pollinators responsible for fertilizing apple, pepper, mango, and cashew plants.

Flies are commonly seen as generalist foragers, lacking nests to provision and often possessing sparsely-haired bodies, which tends to downplay their importance as pollinators. Nevertheless, they can indeed be significant pollinators for specific plant species.

Plants that attract flies include: Sunflowers, dill, parsley, fennel.

Beetles

Beetles reign supreme as the most diverse group of organisms on our planet. Astonishingly, approximately one out of every four described species of plants, animals, bacteria, or fungi is, in fact, a member of the beetle family. Given the vastness of this group, it's no surprise that beetles exhibit a striking array of colors, shapes, and ecological roles.

Plants that attract beetles include: Fennel, mint, butterfly weed, dandelion, marigold, cosmos, dill, Queen Anne's lace, cilantro.

Fossil records offer a glimpse into the past, suggesting that beetles, alongside flies, likely held the role of being the first insect pollinators for prehistoric flowering plants during the late Jurassic era, around 150 million years ago. Remarkably, beetles continue to serve as pollinators for many contemporary flowers, including magnolias and water lilies, which link us to ancient floral forms.

Orchards are not only a vital source of delicious fruits but can also serve as sanctuaries for pollinators crucial to their growth and productivity. Pollinators, such as bees, butterflies, and other insects, play a pivotal role in the pollination of orchard blossoms, ensuring abundant fruit yields. To support these essential partners, it's essential to establish optimal food and nesting sources in orchards.

Nurturing Pollinators in Orchard Landscapes

Orchards are not only a vital source of delicious fruits but can also serve as sanctuaries for pollinators crucial to their growth and productivity. Pollinators, such as bees, butterflies, and other insects, play a pivotal role in the pollination of orchard blossoms, ensuring abundant fruit yields. To support these essential partners, it's essential to establish optimal food and nesting sources in orchards.

Food Sources

Flowering Trees: Orchards can be enriched by planting a variety of flowering trees, not just the fruit-bearing ones. These additional blossoms provide nectar and pollen, sustaining pollinators throughout the growing season.

Native Wildflowers and Herbs: Surrounding orchards with native wildflower meadows or strips can offer a diverse and year-round food source for pollinators. Native plants are adapted to the local ecosystem and are often more attractive to native pollinators.

Cover Crops: Utilizing cover crops like clover and buckwheat in between rows can provide additional nourishment for pollinators, particularly during the periods when fruit trees are not in bloom.

Minimal Pesticide Use: Reducing the use of pesticides and herbicides in orchards can safeguard the health of pollinators by preventing contamination of their food sources. Integrated pest management strategies can help minimize the need for chemicals.

Nesting Sources

Beehives and Bee Boxes: Placing beehives and bee boxes within or near orchards can create suitable nesting sites for solitary and honeybee species. Providing these housing options encourages a stable bee population to assist with pollination.

Wild Bee Habitats: Orchards can include undisturbed areas with deadwood, hollow stems, and sandy patches for ground-nesting bees. These areas can mimic natural bee habitats and promote nesting.

Nesting Tubes: Orchards can install nesting tubes designed for solitary bees. These tubes provide safe spaces for these vital pollinators to lay their eggs and rear their young.

Butterfly Gardens: Including butterfly-friendly plants, host plants for caterpillars, and puddling areas for butterflies in and around orchards can attract and provide suitable habitats for these pollinators.

Creating a holistic environment that addresses both food and nesting sources is essential for the well-being of pollinators in orchards. By supporting their needs, orchard owners not only ensure healthy fruit production but also contribute to the preservation of these essential species that sustain ecosystems and biodiversity.

Tips for Creating a Pollinator-Friendly Environment

Our gardens and orchards are buzzing with life, thanks to the hardworking pollinators that help bring forth the fruits of our labor. Bees, butterflies, and other insects play an indispensable role in the pollination of our favorite plants, ensuring bountiful harvests. To foster a harmonious environment for these essential creatures, it's crucial to adopt practices that make your outdoor space pollinator-friendly.

In this section, we'll explore a few tips on creating a habitat that supports the needs of pollinators, from mindful pest control to nurturing their life cycles and embracing the beauty of natural disorder. By following these guidelines, you can express your gratitude to these unsung heroes of the garden and enjoy the sweet rewards they help produce.

Mindful Pest Control

When dealing with pests like mosquitoes and wasps, be cautious about the chemicals and sprays you use. Some of these substances may harm important pollinators like bees. To avoid unintentionally harming pollinators, always read the label and understand the impact of the products you're using. Furthermore, try to turn to chemical sprays only as a last resort; often, you can effectively manage pests using natural alternatives.For example, you can use citronella to repel mosquitoes.

Support Insect Life Cycles

Butterflies, for instance, rely on specific plants like milkweeds for their survival. They lay their eggs under the leaves, and the caterpillars that hatch must feed on these plants to transform into butterflies. To encourage butterflies to inhabit your area, go beyond just planting milkweed. Keep an eye out for hidden eggs or caterpillars in your garden, and avoid cutting back your plants too aggressively or too early. These actions provide safe spaces for these vital stages of the butterfly's life cycle.

Embrace Natural Disorder

While maintaining a perfectly manicured garden is visually appealing, it's essential to understand that nature can be a bit messy. Fallen leaves, grass clippings, and plants that naturally die back might disrupt the tidy appearance of your garden, but embracing this natural disorder is one of the best things you can do for your local pollinators. Dedicate a portion of your landscape to a more natural, unmanicured state. Leave the leaves and debris alone, allowing wildflowers to grow and naturally recede. This might alter the pristine look of that area, but it will create a thriving habitat for your pollinator friends.

The next time you see a pollinator buzzing around your garden, take a moment to appreciate their valuable service. Without these diligent creatures, our world would be quite different, and the fruit trees we love so much might not thrive. By making your yard a welcoming place for pollinators, you'll be on your way to enjoying bountiful harvests of your favorite fruits.

Hand Pollination

If you've got indoor fruit trees or plants that lack their natural pollinators, such as many tropical species, it might be time to step into the role of a pollinator yourself. Hand-pollination is the key to ensuring that pollen is effectively distributed and increasing your chances of a fruitful harvest.

Here's how to hand-pollinate flowers:

- **Locate the Open Flowers:** Identify flowers that have opened, and look for the telltale yellow pollen. Keep in mind that some flowers have both male and female parts, so you may need to check multiple blooms to locate the pollen.

- **Choose Your Tool:** Grab a small tool for the job, like a cotton swab, a fine paintbrush, or even your fingertip.

- **Collect and Transfer Pollen:** Gently collect the pollen using your tool, and then carefully swirl it around the flowers' reproductive parts. If you have multiple plants, make sure to visit each one. Remember, think like a bee—be gentle and thorough, visiting every flower to ensure you don't miss any.

- **Repeat the Process:** Continue this hand-pollination process every few days until the tree or plant is no longer in bloom.

By becoming a pollinator on your own land, you'll take an active role in supporting fruit production, ensuring that your indoor garden thrives and bears the fruits of your labor.

The Takeaway

Without proper pollination, it's impossible to have a bountiful harvest. Fruit trees are either self-pollinating or cross-pollinating. Self-pollinating trees produce fruit that is exactly the same as the previous generations. The quality and taste of the produce may not meet the desired characteristics. Cross-pollination provides more variety and higher chances of creating fruit with superior characteristics.

Attracting beneficial insects that could serve as pollinators is an effective way to increase harvest. Installing nesting tubes, bee boxes, and planting clovers as cover crops can draw a significant number of bees, birds, and beetles to your orchard. Lastly, it's important to create a pollinator-friendly environment by being mindful of chemical methods of pest control and supporting insect life cycles. If all else fails, you can always go for hand pollination.

CHAPTER 8

Harvest Management and Winter Care

You've done all the heavy lifting. You planted your orchard, nurtured your plants, encouraged pollination, and enhanced fruit production. All your efforts have paid off and your trees are laden with fruits ready to be picked. How do you go about harvesting? As your garden thrives, how do you manage dense tree canopies? And, most importantly, what do you do with all that harvest? In this chapter, we'll cover all these questions and more because, as it turns out, setting up a successful orchard is only the beginning of an exciting adventure.

Thinning Top-Heavy Trees

Thinning fruit trees at this stage might seem counterintuitive, but there are compelling reasons to do so. At first glance, the idea of plucking young, unripe fruit may seem at odds with your goal of growing a bountiful crop. However, thinning fruit trees not only works in your favor but also contributes to the long-term health of your orchard. In this section, we'll delve into the reasons behind thinning your fruit trees, as well as when and how to do it.

Advantages of Thinning Fruit Trees

- Mitigate overbearing and prevent early fruit drop
- Enhance the size, color, and quality of remaining fruit
- Safeguard tree limbs from damage due to heavy fruit loads
- Encourage the development of next year's crop and mitigate biennial bearing

A Simple Guide to Thinning Fruit Trees

Thinning fruit trees is a straightforward task that requires only your fingers or a small pair of sharp pruners. However, timing is key. To effectively thin out fruit trees, it's crucial to act during the right window. This window opens after pollination has occurred and in the early phases of fruit development, typically when the young fruit is still under an inch in diameter. In most regions, thinning your fruit trees is typically no longer necessary after July. Now let's look at individual trees and how you should approach thinning.

Apple

The ideal timing for thinning apple trees is approximately one month after the peak of their blooming period. During the thinning process, it's essential to disperse any fruit clusters, leaving only one, well-selected fruit behind. Generally, it's advisable to retain the fruit from the "king bloom," which is the middle blossom within the flower cluster, as it holds the greatest potential for growing into a robust and sizable apple. Maintain a spacing of about six to eight inches between the remaining fruit.

For spur-type apple trees, fruit formation occurs on spurs located along the inner limbs, bearing fruit from the trunk outward. In some cases, thinning may be required to promote the development of larger and higher-quality fruit on the remaining spurs.

Apricot

Apricot trees are renowned for their high productivity, which can lead to fruit drop if the trees are not properly thinned. It's essential to disperse fruit clusters throughout the tree and maintain a distance of approximately six inches between the remaining fruits to mitigate this issue.

Cherry

Normally, sweet cherry and sour cherry trees don't require thinning of their fruit. However, if your trees are experiencing fruit drop due to stress, it may be advisable to consider thinning a portion of the fruit. It's recommended to limit the number of cherries on any single spur to no more than ten. Therefore, you should thin out any clusters that are causing crowding issues or contributing to the problem of cherry drop.

Peach

These fruit trees are wellknown for their tendency to overproduce, which, in turn, often necessitates regular thinning to prevent potential damage to the tree. As these fruits ripen, they can become quite heavy, posing a risk of limb breakage and bark tearing if the tree is allowed to bear this weight. It's essential to disperse both fruit clusters and any 'twins' that may form. Maintain a minimum of six inches of spacing between the remaining fruits to ensure the tree's health and longevity.

Pear

Pear trees, whether of the Asian or European variety, typically do not demand thinning. However, if you observe a pattern of premature fruit drop while the pears are still small and unripe, or if your tree tends to produce fruit every other year, thinning can serve as an effective solution. Swiftly remove any undersized, misshapen, or damaged fruit as soon as it emerges. Disperse clusters of fruit, retaining just one to two fruits from each cluster to enhance the size of the mature fruit. Ensure a spacing of approximately four to six inches between the remaining fruit for optimal results.

Plum

Japanese plum trees share a reputation for overproduction and fruit drop similar to nectarine and peach trees. These trees commonly bear fruit in clusters along the branches. Once the plums have reached a sufficient size for easy harvesting, it's advisable to thin them out and disperse the clusters. This practice allows the fruit to grow to a larger size and helps prevent premature fruit drop. Maintain a spacing of approximately four to six inches between the remaining fruit.

European plum trees typically require less thinning compared to their Japanese counterparts. However, if your European plum tree produces mature but undersized fruit due to overbearing, thinning the fruit may be beneficial for enhancing the size of the remaining fruit in the future. Leave single fruits with a two to three inch gap between them, or keep pairs of fruit with a six-inch separation.

Bringing in the Harvest!

Finally, we've reached our destination: ripe fruit. We waited patiently, monitoring the subtle day-to-day changes in each fruit as it neared this moment. Sweet, flavorful, aromatic, boasting ideal texture, and harvested at its peak, it stands in a class of its own. It is unrivaled by anything you might find at the farmers' market, a local farm stand, the grocery store, or even a high-end mail-order service.

Home gardeners enjoy the unique privilege of tending to individual trees, meticulously pruning year-round, thinning excess, mulching, watering, and nurturing them when they're faced with pest challenges and diseases. This is why homegrown fruits nears perfection. Commercial growers, no matter how skilled and dedicated, can't match the personalized care a home gardener provides.

With time and experience, you develop an instinct for recognizing ripe fruit, making harvesting an intuitive process. The goal of fruit trees is reproduction. Fruits, typically containing seeds or pits, entice animals, including humans, to carry them away and spread them to new areas. When the fruit is ripe and ready for this journey, it naturally detaches from the tree.

Apples

Sometimes fruits may appear ripe, but don't pluck them just yet. Last year, I made the mistake of harvesting Fuji apples in my orchard because of their enticing color. In doing so, I missed out on a far more exquisite flavor that I could've experienced if I waited just three more weeks.

In many cases, fruits that lack the required taste, haven't had the chance to develop their full sweetness and the richness of their flavor. Some apple varieties, like Ashmead's Kernel, require even more time to mature and reach their peak flavor with proper storage.

A simple test to check for ripeness is to give the fruit a gentle tug. Apples will break from their branches almost instantly.

Apricots

Growers often pick them before they ripen to prevent bruising. While apricots do continue to ripen somewhat off the tree, they never achieve the same level of sweetness as they would on the branch. Compared to other fruits, apricots usually ripen at the same time, creating a short window of time to harvest them. Bright golden orange color is an indication the fruit has reached its prime. It feels soft to the touch and you can check whether it's ready by pressing your thumb.

Figs

They're just as fragile as apricots; however, they stop ripening once they're off the trees. You won't get maximum flavor if you pick a fig too soon. Filled with rich, plump sugars, ripened figs bend the branches. Limp, drooping stems are a sign that the fruit hanging from their tips is ready for harvest. Figs tend to drop by themselves from the branches.

Search for drooping branches and give each fruit a gentle squeeze. If the fruit feels soft and breaks easily from its stem, then it's ready to harvest. Figs tend to taste better as they degrade a little. You can even allow them to dry on trees, letting them shrivel at the stem or placing them on a drying rack somewhere safe from insects and animals.

Cherries/Plums/Peaches/Nectarines

In stone fruits, deepening of color, aroma and tender feel is usually an indication of ripeness. However, leaving the fruit on the trees for too long can result in the formation of translucent areas in the flesh known as "water core." These are caused by the accumulation of sugars, usually due to a heat spell. Look out for fallen fruit or two at the base of these trees. It's a sign that fruits are ready for harvesting. With experience, you can tell if a particular stone fruit is ripe just by touching it.. Leave the fruits that feel firm on the tree. The flesh of ripened stone fruits also peels easily. Peaches and nectarines become extremely fragrant when they're ready for harvest.

Pears

Unlike most fruits, pears don't achieve the best quality if they're left on the trees to ripen. For best results, pick them when they're mature but not ripe. To harvest, gently tug the fruit until it separates from the stem. Avoid pulling or twisting. If it doesn't break easily, let it remain on the trees for a few more days.

Summer pear varieties like Bartlett will be ready for harvest in early August. Their color brightens, the longer they stay attached to the trees. Pick them off the branches as they begin to color and store in a cool place, preferably below 75°F. A vibrant yellow color indicates softer, sweeter fruit. Depending on what you prefer, harvest once the pears have achieved the required color. Keep ripe Bartletts in the refrigerator for a day or two.

Winter pears such as Anjou, Bosc, and Comice usually ripen in September. They may require chilled storage at below 40°F for up to two to six weeks. The shelf life of pears is a lot shorter compared to apples and since they ripen from the inside out, it's difficult to prevent rotting until it's too late. The best time to eat a pear is when the outer flesh gives away to gentle pressure.

Storing Your Produce

Some fruit varieties are known for their limited storage life. Typically, these include early-cropping apples and pears, as well as most stone fruit. These fruits have thinner skins, and higher juice and sugar content, which makes them prone to spoilage if left as whole fruit at room temperature. They tend to deteriorate within a week or two. To prolong the freshness of these fruits without processing, the best option is to store them in the salad drawer of your refrigerator. At approximately 4°C, you can expect to store even early apple varieties like Discovery for three or four weeks before they become soft and mealy.

Late-season apples and certain winter pears, such as GlouMorceau, can be successfully stored as whole fruit using the traditional method of wrapping them in newspaper and placing them in trays. To ensure they last as long as possible, there are a few tips you can follow. First, only store perfect fruit. Any with skin blemishes or windfalls should be used promptly and kept separate from the unblemished ones to prevent the spread of mold and brown rot. Choose a storage location that is cool, dry, and dark, with a garage being an ideal option due to the need for constant cool temperatures. Regularly inspect the fruit and remove any that show signs of deterioration.

One of the reasons Bramley cooking apples are popular is due to their long shelf life. They can be stored as whole fruit until April or May of the following year. However, in modern times, freezing fruit has become a quicker and simpler preservation method.

For cooking apples, simply stew them with a bit of water and sugar, allow them to cool in the pan, and then transfer them into freezer bags, labeling them before placing them in your freezer. This method is highly recommended over the traditional newspaper and box approach, as it allows you to grow various early varieties with great flavor but shorter storage lives.

Another effective method is to freeze thin slices. This works well for dessert apples, which, due to their higher sugar content, do not turn to mush when cooked. After peeling, coring, and thinly slicing the fruit, dip the slices into a bowl of water with lemon juice to prevent browning. You can also use a mixture of pineapple juice and lemon juice, which adds extra flavor to the apple slices. Arrange the slices on a parchment-lined baking sheet and place them in the quick freeze section of your freezer. After a couple of hours, when the slices are frozen, transfer them to a freezer bag, label it, and return it to the freezer.

Of course, there are numerous other methods for preserving your harvest, including juicing, making jam, canning, and drying. And don't forget the classic technique of steeping fruit in alcohol. So when the stores are filled with fruit that has been shipped from far away, you can enjoy the bounty from your own garden.

DIY Apple Storage Rack

An ingenious method to store apples for a considerably long time is to keep them in an apple storage rack. It reaches a height of five feet. So you can easily peer into the top drawer and extend my reach all the way to the back. Every drawer has the capacity to accommodate approximately 40 large apples, including those hefty Honeycrisps weighing in at half a pound each. With a total of ten drawers, that's 200 pounds of apples or an impressive 400 sizable ones (or even more if they're smaller). This quantity is just right to sustain my family of four throughout a chilly Vermont winter.

Here's how you can build your own apple storage rack:
- Start by building the side rails (drawer glides) using 1x3 dimensional lumber.

- Cut 5 ft uprights from the 1x3 lumber and lay them out before attaching 11 pieces of 1x3 wood at 30 inches long.
- Adjust the depth of the rack as needed, 30 inches is quite deep.
- Ensure the drawer glide spacing is level and evenly spaced for smooth sliding.
- The drawers will be sided with 1x2 boards, and a spare 1x3 board works well as a spacer for the drawer glides.
- Optionally, add two more vertical supports to each side for stability.
- Attach the sides together to form a box.
- Use 30-inch top and bottom side trim boards on the outside.
- Add trim pieces (23 3/4 inches) on the front and back, overlapping the side trim boards.
- Finish the top with 10 top slats cut to 23 3/4 inches, spaced 1/2 inch apart.
- The box for the rack is complete, now build the drawers.
- Start by building a box from 1x2 dimensional lumber, which will serve as the edge supports of each drawer.
- The drawer sides are 30 inches, and the fronts are 19 inches.
- Pre-drill holes to avoid splitting the wood and use appropriate screws or a nail gun for assembly.
- Attach drawer slats across the bottom, running from front to back.
- Each drawer will need 7 slats, spaced 1/2 inch apart to allow airflow and prevent items from falling through.
- Repeat the process to build all the drawers.
- Once the drawers are made, remove them to make the rack easier to move.
- The finished rack is large, but it can be carried by one person when empty.

Figure 28: Apple storage rack.

Winter Care

Ensuring the safety of fruit tree root systems during winter is essential for winterizing your fruit trees. The goal is to safeguard the tree's delicate feeder roots, known as root hairs, against freezing temperatures. These fine roots are responsible for absorbing vital water and nutrients from the soil. In freezing conditions, these feeder roots can be at risk of frost damage, jeopardizing the tree's capacity to access the necessary moisture and nutrients, ultimately resulting in tree stress. In severe cases, an affected tree may even succumb.

Protective measures include insulating the root system effectively by applying a layer of mulch around the tree's base. Mulch acts as a protective shield against the harsh winter cold, providing a vital defense for the feeder roots. Various mulch materials are available, such as wood chips or straw, each with its advantages and disadvantages. However, make sure to avoid using compost or decomposed manure in the fall, as these nutrient-rich mulches can stimulate the tree's growth, potentially delaying its dormancy.

Shielding the tree trunk from winter sunscald is necessary to protect against temperature-induced harm, especially on the southwest side of the tree where sunlight exposure is most significant. The rationale behind this practice revolves around understanding the effects of temperature fluctuations on the tree. In the daytime, the tree's trunk expands as it absorbs sunlight-generated warmth. However, rapid cooling at night causes the bark to contract swiftly.

When the bark loses flexibility due to these temperature shifts, it can develop cracks or fissures, leaving the tree vulnerable to cold and creating an entry point for pests and disease. This risk is exacerbated if there is snow on the ground because the snow reflects and amplifies sunlight, intensifying temperature fluctuations and elevating the risk of sun scald.

During winter, young and recently planted trees are also susceptible to wildlife damage. With reduced food sources available to them during the winter months, rabbits and rodents may find the tender young bark of fruit trees especially appealing when the weather turns cold.

To safeguard your tree against sun scald, apply a protective layer of a mixture consisting of 50% white latex paint (even leftover house paint will suffice) and 50% water to the trunk. This white coating acts as a barrier against winter sun damage. Alternatively, you can utilize white plastic spiral tree guards or wrap the trunk with kitchen foil, both of which serve as effective deterrents against rabbit and rodent damage as well. However, remember to remove these plastic tree guards or foil in early spring to prevent potential pest breeding underneath.

The Takeaway

When your trees start producing fruit, that's when the true labor starts. Harvesting fruits at the right time is the key to achieving the best quality. The signs of ripening vary for different fruits. Some need to remain attached to the tree to acquire the best flavor while others should be picked before they ripen. Once the fruit is off the trees, it's time to store the excess. Storage options range from simply refrigerating to creating jams, chutneys, or canning. The final stage of managing your orchard involves taking care of your trees during winter. Mulching, using tree guards, or painting white latex on the tree trunks are some effective ways to minimize the damage as the temperatures drop.

CONCLUSION

The Adventure Never Ends

I want to extend my heartfelt appreciation to you for embarking on this journey of fruit tree cultivation. Your dedication and passion for growing your backyard orchard are commendable, and I'm grateful to have been a part of your learning process. As you reach the final pages of this book, I want to emphasize the value of maintaining a curious and open-minded approach to your fruit tree endeavors. Remember that your orchard is an ever-evolving canvas, and there's always more to discover. Your journey is far from over; it's a lifelong exploration of the world of fruit trees.

I encourage you to continue experimenting, pushing boundaries, and embracing the joy of discovery. Explore new fruit varieties that pique your interest, experiment with innovative techniques, and dare to think outside the box. Fruit tree cultivation is not just a science; it's an art that thrives on your creativity and willingness to take risks.

To help you in your ongoing research, I've compiled a list of valuable resources and references that you can turn to for further guidance and inspiration. I encourage you to check out the other books in this series: *The Practical Permaculture Project* and *Beginner's Guide to Successful Container Gardening*. You can also visit my website: https://SmartMindPublishing.com/ where you'll find loads of useful tips as well as my workbook titled *My Guided Fruit Tree Garden Planner* to help you on your home gardening journey.

In closing, I hope you'll carry the spirit of curiosity and experimentation with you as you tend to your orchard. Your dedication to learning, your love for the fruit, and your willingness to embrace both successes and failures will undoubtedly lead to a bountiful harvest and a deeper connection with your fruit trees.

Thank you for sharing this journey with me, and may your orchard continue to flourish and delight for years to come!

Thanks for Reading,
Please Leave a Review!

I would be *incredibly appreciative* if you could rate my book or leave a review on **Amazon**.

Just scan this QR code with your phone, or visit the www.ftg.sophiemckay.com link to land directly on the book's Amazon review page.

Your review not only helps me create better books, but also helps more fellow gardener experience success in the garden and put healthy food on their family's table.

Thank you!

Sophie

What to Read Next?

If You Liked This Book, Try These Ones Too!

Check out Sophie's books to keep your garden thriving all year round. Create your own sustainable permaculture garden, or dive deep into container gardening with proven DIY methods for composting, companion planting, seed saving, water management and pest control!

Sophie McKay's Easy and Effective Gardneing Series

Enhance Your Gardening Journey with Sophie's Garden Planners!

 Just scan this QR code with your phone, or use the link to land directly on the book's Amazon page,

or

 Visit the Author's bookstore at www.smartmindpublishing.com

Bibliography

Adding Fruit to Your Homestead. (n.d.). Stark Bros. Retrieved July 1, 2023

All About Tree Stakes. (n.d.). Stark Bros. Retrieved July 14, 2023,

Anderson, C. (2023, February 23). *Soaker Hose vs Drip Irrigation: Which Irrigation System Is Better?* Sweet New Earth. Retrieved July 21, 2023.

Anderson, C. (2023, February 23). *Soaker Hose vs Drip Irrigation: Which Irrigation System Is Better?* Sweet New Earth. Retrieved July 23, 2023.

Baker, N. (2023, February 27). *Our Guide to the USDA Gardening Zones—Plus, the Best Plants to Grow in Your Region*. Martha Stewart. Retrieved June 30, 2023.

BC Fruit Tree Production Guide. (n.d.). *Fruit Tree Nutrition*. BC Tree Fruit Production Guide. Retrieved July 26, 2023.

Benefits of a South Facing Garden & House. (2017, September 19). Barratt Homes. Retrieved June 28, 2023.

Chilling requirement. (n.d.). Wikipedia. Retrieved June 30, 2023.

Choosing a Tree at a Tree Nursery | What is a Nursery Tree? (n.d.). Richard's Tree Service. Retrieved July 10, 2023.

Clark, J. (2007). *Light Brown Apple Moth in California*. UC IPM.

Climate Zones and Chill Hours. (n.d.). Tomorrow's Harvest by Burchell Nursery. Retrieved June 30, 2023.

da Silva, C. (n.d.). *The Importance of Soil Testing - Stark Bro's*. Stark Bros. Retrieved July 3, 2023.

Designing a fruit tree guild – Lakeside Community Garden. (n.d.). Lakeside Community Garden. Retrieved September 28, 2023.

Establishing a Home Orchard. (2015, February 4). Backyard Gardener.

Fruit Tree Nutrition. (n.d.). BC Tree Fruit Production Guide. Retrieved July 24, 2023, from https://www.bctfpg.ca/horticulture/fruit-tree-nutrition/

Gaines, M. (2023, May 3). *Fruit Trees 101: Pollination – FastGrowingTrees.com*. Fast Growing Trees. Retrieved October 29, 2023.

George Silva. (2018, May 8). *What organic fertilizers mean to plants and soil*. Michigan State University.

Grant, A. (2023, March 22). *Beneficial Nematodes For Gardening - How Do Beneficial Nematodes Work*. Gardening Know How.

A Guide to Buying Fruit Trees - bare root or containerised? (n.d.). R.V.Roger Ltd. Retrieved July 12, 2023.

Harmon, D. (2023, July 3). *What Is Inorganic Fertilizer?* HomeQuestionsAnswered. Retrieved July 26, 2023.

Harris, N. (2022, March). *Companion Planting*. WVU Extension.

How to stake a tree. (n.d.). Space for Life. Retrieved July 15, 2023.

Kidd, E. (n.d.). *The Importance of Fruit Tree Pollination*. Stark Bro's. Retrieved October 27, 2023.

Laritson, W. (2022, March 31). *How Much Sun Do Fruit Trees Need? | Naturehills.com*. Nature Hills Nursery. Retrieved June 27, 2023, from https://www.naturehills.com/blog/post/how-much-sun-do-fruit-trees-need

McDowell, S. (2022, December 9). *The Simple Art of Grafting Fruit Trees: A Complete Guide*. Orchard People. .

Microclimates: assessing your garden. (n.d.). RHS. Retrieved June 28, 2023.

Nature Hills. (2020, April 29). *Fruit Tree Tips*. Nature Hills Nursery. Retrieved October 15, 2023.

Perfect Plants. (2021, September 21). *Pollination in Fruit Trees*. Perfect Plants. Retrieved October 27, 2023.

Planning a Wholesale Orchard. (n.d.). Stark Bros. Retrieved July 2, 2023.

Planting Fruit Trees. (n.d.). The Old Farmer's Almanac. Retrieved July 13, 2023.

Ralph, A. (2015). *Grow a Little Fruit Tree: Simple Pruning Techniques for Small-Space, Easy-Harvest Fruit Trees*. Storey Publishing, LLC.

Ralph, A. (2015). *Grow a Little Fruit Tree: Simple Pruning Techniques for Small-Space, Easy-Harvest Fruit Trees*. Storey Publishing, LLC.

RHS. (n.d.). *Trees: growing in containers*. RHS. Retrieved October 27, 2023.

Roger, R. V. (2020). *A Guide to Harvesting and Storing Fruit*. R.V.Roger Ltd. Retrieved November 6, 2023.

Seifrit, D. (2023, March 9). *Beginning Grower: Planning and Planting an Orchard*. Penn State Extension. Retrieved July 2, 2023.

Stark, A. (2018). *4 Benefits of Thinning Fruit Trees*. Stark Bro's. Retrieved November 4, 2023.

Stark, R. (2019). *Winter Protection for Fruit Trees*. Stark Bro's. Retrieved November 7, 2023.

Stark, T. (n.d.). *More Pollinators and More Nitrogen: Planting Clover Cover Crops in Your Orchard*. Stark Bro's. Retrieved October 28, 2023.

Stark Bros. (n.d.). *Fertilizing Organic Fruit Trees*. Stark Bros. Retrieved July 25, 2023.

Stross, A. (2023, June 15). *How to Build a Permaculture Fruit Tree Guild*. Tenth Acre Farm. Retrieved October 14, 2023.

Urban Farmstead. (2021, May 9). *How to Plant, Prune, and Irrigate Fruit Trees EVERYTHING YOU NEED TO KNOW*. YouTube. Retrieved June 26, 2023.

Von Rosenberg, S. (2015, May 14). *Fruit Trees and Water*. UC ANR. Retrieved July 19, 2023.

Watson, T. (n.d.). *Optimize Your Fruit Trees' Soil for Optimal Health & Harvest!* Gardening Calendar. Retrieved July 3, 2023.

What Are Chill Hours and How Do You Count Them? Fruit Tree Care. (2023, February 4). Grow Organic. Retrieved June 30, 2023.

What is a Food Forest? (n.d.). Project Food Forest. Retrieved October 15, 2023.

What is a rootstock? Its types & uses. (n.d.). Orchardly. Retrieved July 12, 2023.

Winger, J. (2022, November 2). *Planning an Orchard for Your Homestead*. The Prairie Homestead. Retrieved June 26, 2023.

Winger, J. (2023, February 20). *What We Learned by Having Our Garden Soil Tested • The Prairie Homestead*. The Prairie Homestead. Retrieved June 26, 2023.

Woods, T. (2014, June 15). *Restore those old fruit trees*. OSU Extension Service. Retrieved August 7, 2023.

Xerces Society. (2023). *Who Are the Pollinators?* Xerces Society. Retrieved October 29, 2023.

www.ingramcontent.com/pod-product-compliance
Lightning Source LLC
Chambersburg PA
CBHW030116100526
44591CB00009B/421